Anti-Judaism in Christian Theology

CHARLOTTE KLEIN

Anti-Judaism in Christian Theology

Translated by Edward Quinn

Fortress Press
Philadelphia

This book is a translation of
Theologie und Anti-Judaismus by Charlotte Klein,
© 1975 Chr. Kaiser Verlag, München,
and is published with the permission of that publisher.

Chapter 7 ('A Short Survey of Anglo-American Authors') and
the Select Bibliography were prepared in English by the author.

First American edition by Fortress Press 1978

Translation and new material
© 1978 The Society for Promoting Christian Knowledge, London,
and Fortress Press, Philadelphia.

Library of Congress Catalog Card Number 76–62600

6200J77   Printed in the United States of America   1–488

Contents

Acknowledgements

Thanks are due to the following for permission to quote from copyright sources:

Abingdon Press: *History of Israelite Religion* by Georg Fohrer (by permission also of SPCK)

A. & C. Black Ltd: *The History of Israel* by Martin Noth (by permission also of Vandenhoeck and Ruprecht); and *The New Testament Era* by Bo Reicke (by permission also of Fortress Press)

Burns & Oates Ltd: *Who is a Christian?* by Hans Urs von Balthasar (by permission also of Paulist–Newman Press); *On the Ruins of the Temple* by Joseph Bonsirven; and *The Relevance of the New Testament* by Heinrich Schlier (by permission also of Herder Freiburg)

Darton, Longman & Todd Ltd: *Jesus and the Gospel*, vol. ii, by Pierre Benoit, translated by B. Weatherhead, copyright © 1974 by Darton, Longman & Todd Ltd (by permission also of The Seabury Press); *Invitation to the New Testament* by W. D. Davies, copyright © 1966 by William D. Davies (by permission also of Doubleday & Co., Inc.); *The Living World of the New Testament* (US title *Understanding the New Testament*) by H. C. Kee and F. W. Young, copyright © Prentice-Hall, Inc., Englewood Cliffs, New Jersey, 1957 (by permission also of Prentice-Hall, Inc.)

Harper & Row, Publishers, Inc.: *Jesus of Nazareth* by Günther Bornkamm

George G. Harrap & Co. Ltd: *A History of Hebrew Civilization* by Alfred Bertholet

Interpretation: 'The Interpretation of the New Testament', part 3, 'Promise and Fulfilment' by Walther Zimmerli, in *Interpretation*, vol. 15 (July 1961), pp. 310–38, reprinted in *Essays on Old Testament Hermeneutics* (UK title *Essays on Old Testament Interpretation*), edited by Claus Westermann, published by John Knox Press and SCM Press (by permission also of SCM Press)

Longman Group Ltd: *The Lord* by Romano Guardini

Anti-Judaism in Christian Theology

Foreword

Behind the straightforward and obvious aims of a religion or culture, we are now increasingly aware of hidden trends which exercise a powerful influence on society and sustain the authority of existing institutions. We all know today that every religion—and therefore also Christianity—can and does contain ideological features. But these features are so closely interwoven with the true content and have often so affected our inherited consciousness of our religion that it is not easy to see how they have distorted the original message. Intelligence and good will are not sufficient here. For most people it becomes possible to discover the ideological influences in their religion only when these find expression in a great and terrible historical happening where their destructive power is too obvious to go unnoticed.

The hatred and persecution of Jews in Hitler's Germany, leading to the extermination camps in the east, were a terrifying racial-pagan phenomenon which had nothing directly to do with religion. But at the same time it is clear that this terrible event, surpassing all that could be imagined, would not have been possible if hostility to the Jews had not been fostered by Christian preaching which spoke of Jews and Judaism almost from the beginning only in terms of rejection. There were some Christians who recognized this at once when Hitler came to power. We may recall Erik Peterson's *Die Kirche aus Juden und Heiden*, which appeared in 1933, and James Parkes' *The Conflict between the Church and the Synagogue* in 1934. These authors tried to make people more aware of the anti-Jewish trends in Christian preaching and at the same time to provide a corrective, presenting the Jews in a more positive light from the standpoint of the Christian faith.

After the war and the extermination of six million Jews,

Christian study groups in many countries began to examine the hatred of Jews displayed in Christian literature. It soon became clear that anti-Jewish ideology is much more deeply rooted in Christian preaching and even in some parts of the New Testament than had once been thought. Pope John XXIII demanded from the Vatican Council a declaration on Jewish-Christian relationships which would provide guidelines for preaching and religious instruction and enable Christians to get rid of the anti-Jewish ideology. The Vatican declaration was only a beginning. Since then in many countries catechisms and textbooks have been re-edited and a different approach adopted in theological works. Christians are no longer interested in presenting Judaism as a degenerate religion, describing the Pharisees as legalists and hypocrites, making the Jewish people responsible for the crucifixion, concealing the Jewish origin of Jesus, Mary, the disciples, and the early Church as a whole; nor do they want to represent the Synagogue as forsaken by God, to speak of the Jews as a people cursed by God. Christians will no longer tolerate preaching of the gospel which becomes a caricature of Judaism, leads to contempt for the Jews, and seems to authorize the unjust treatment of Jews.

Despite these efforts on the part of ecclesiastical authorities and some theologians, not much in the Church has really changed. This at any rate is the opinion of theologians who have dealt with the problem. The present book again raises the question of how people in the Christian Church today think and speak of Jews. Has there been any criticism of the ideology which prevailed up to Auschwitz? Or do people speak as they always did? Are at least theologians and students of theology now aware of the fact that they may speak of the Jews only in a responsible fashion and should avoid any expressions which foster contempt for the Jewish people? Or do Christian teachers no longer think of Auschwitz when they are talking about Jews? Is Auschwitz something which is of no concern to the Christian Church in Germany?

The anti-Jewish trend is more deeply rooted in Christianity than might at first be supposed. That is why the efforts of the Vatican Council and other ecclesiastical authorities have had so little success. For it is very difficult to eliminate from the proclamation of the gospel a negation of the Jewish people. The proclamation of Jesus as the Messiah in whom all the divine promises have been fulfilled seems to leave no scope for a religion which finds that the presence of the Messiah is not credible in a world filled with hate and violence and which therefore feels bound to wait for a while yet for the messianic age. Consequently it is not easy to proclaim Jesus Christ without at the same time implying a negation of the Jews. As the Church, we see ourselves as the chosen people replacing the Jewish people, which by its infidelity is considered to have set itself outside the divine covenant. This is what Matthew's Gospel already clearly states. Can we be surprised that the mental negation of Jewish existence was turned into a legal and political negation as soon as the Church entered into the victorious cultural complex of the ancient world?

Must the Christian message then for ever remain anti-Jewish? Or is the negation of Jewish existence an ideological distortion of the truth of salvation which the Church was able to discover only after Auschwitz? Here opinions differ. There are, however, theologians today who think that the anti-Jewish trend in Christianity will not be overcome as long as the Church does not take biblical eschatology seriously, does not long for the return of the Lord, and thus does not more clearly recognize the evil of the present time. Only when we consistently refuse in our religious statements to separate Jesus from his coming kingdom and do not claim for the present time what is promised only for the consummation do we allow scope for those who are waiting, for the Jews and other peoples; only then do we avoid the temptation of claiming for the Church today titles of sovereignty which belong to it only in the light of the end-time.

GREGORY BAUM
St Michael's College
University of Toronto

1
Introduction

More than fifty years ago G. F. Moore, a well-known American specialist in Jewish studies, wrote an article in the *Harvard Theological Review* which he called 'Christian Writers on Judaism'.[1] In this investigation of over fifty pages, which still made no claim to be exhaustive, Moore observed that Christian interest in Jewish literature had always been apologetic or polemical rather than historical. Christian writers wanted to prove that Jesus was the Messiah expected in the Jewish Bible and that he was the Son of God. Other important themes in their work included 'the emancipation of Christians from the Mosaic law, or the annulment of the dispensation of law altogether, or the substitution of the new law of Christ; the repudiation of the Jewish people by God for their rejection of Christ, and the succession of the Church, the true Israel, the people of God, to all the prerogatives and promises once given to the Jews'.[2]

In the second part of his article—the first deals with works from the second to the eighteenth century—the author considers the writings of his contemporaries. 'These later authors would have described their aim as historical—to exhibit the beliefs and teachings of Judaism in New Testament times or in the early centuries of the Christian era. For this purpose they employed chiefly the material that came down from their predecessors, without giving sufficient consideration to the fact that it had been gathered for every conceivable motive except to serve as material for the historian . . . A delectus of quotations made for a polemic purpose is the last kind of a source to which a historian would go to get a just notion of what a religion really was to its adherents.'[3]

Over half a century divides us from Moore's exposition. The last authors whose work he mentioned were Emil Schürer and

Wilhelm Bousset, both Germans; their books, constantly appearing in new editions, have exercised an almost incalculable influence on generations of New Testament scholars. Here we have to ask about the situation in our own times: how far has the presentation of Judaism, criticized by Moore in the light of the works then available, been changed in publications from 1921 to the present day? Or has it perhaps remained the same?

First of all, something must be said about the literature with which we are concerned here. While Moore could still call his article 'Christian Writers on Judaism', a distinction must be made today: there is a whole series of objective Christian presentations of Judaism, in almost all European languages and on all levels, which sincerely attempt to do justice to their theme.[4] These works, aiming simply and directly at a presentation of Judaism as such, are outside the scope of the present book. Here we are considering only those authors who describe Christianity, its origins and theology, its relationship to what we know as the Old Testament, and who consequently could not avoid discussing Jewish ideas and parties and the situation of Jewry in the early Christian centuries. Often enough their books can be described as histories of New Testament times, but these are not the only works which had to include some treatment of the question of Judaism. Hence our inquiry will include a large number of studies which deal with Judaism, Jewish life and ideas in the centuries before and after the beginning of the Christian era; either because they introduce the reader to the Old or New Testament in terms of the history of the times, of exegesis, or of theology, or because they seek to provide an insight into the origin of the Gospels and thus also into the contemporary Jewish milieu.

Special importance has been attached to books published for the first time or going into new editions in the last decade, which for that reason are probably the most widely read. Not that the work of earlier authors could be entirely ignored. For one thing, their books continue to enjoy a scarcely diminished authority, partly because they are by well-known scholars and partly because the material contained in them (for example, Strack/Billerbeck) is in fact nowhere else found in such

2

abundance and in such a manageable form. Another reason for going back to the older authors is the fact that the moderns also constantly adopt the same procedure; many of them do not present any new material compiled independently from Jewish sources, and the writers of the sixties have a way of referring back to the books of their predecessors in earlier decades, continuing to cite these as authoritative.

It must also be emphasized that we are concerned with works intended mainly for students of theology in universities and colleges. On the whole therefore neither books of a popular character nor those directly intended for religious instruction in schools are considered. An investigation of the catechetical material in Germany would certainly be useful and some attempts have been made in this field,[5] but they have not produced anything up to the standard of the scrupulously exact and scholarly surveys undertaken in France, England, Belgium, the United States, and even in Italy and Spain. From a superficial analysis in Germany the conclusion was drawn that this material contained nothing anti-Semitic, and people were content to leave it at that.

Our investigation is concerned mainly with books in German, but some French works relating to the same theme have also been brought in for purposes of comparison. There are several reasons for looking mainly at German works. It was not by chance that G. F. Moore already in 1921, in the article mentioned above, quoted almost exclusively German-speaking authors among his contemporaries and sharply criticized their presentation of Judaism. He accused them of an inadequate, one-sided selection of Jewish sources, an *a priori* biased attitude towards those sources, and objected to their continual use of a method of comparison which tended to depreciate everything Jewish and to upvalue everything Christian at the expense of the former. It may be stated, however, that this is not generally the case in the English-speaking countries; although there is no time or space for proving this at length, a brief chapter has been added on the state of affairs in these countries. It is a question of fundamental and not merely quantitative differences. A comparative study would be appropriate and informative in this respect. It would ascertain the causes of the differences in the treatment of the same theme: differences which can be observed, for example, between John Lightfoot and Johann Christoph Wagenseil in the seventeenth century up to W. D. Davies and Martin Noth in our own time. Among the causes of the negative judgement on Judaism in Germany may well be for one thing Luther's hostility to the 'law' and 'works'. But some part has also been played by the general cultural and political attitude to contemporary Judaism: an attitude which on the Continent right up to the present time has always been different from that of the English-speaking world.

Both Protestant and Catholic authors are quoted here. If more Protestant authors are mentioned, this is due to the fact that until almost thirty years ago there was scarcely any independent Catholic biblical study, and Catholic scholars in this field are therefore less numerous than their Protestant colleagues. For some time also, at least at university level, scarcely any distinction has been made in the use of works by Catholic or Protestant scholars. Both therefore are cited indiscriminately here, although occasionally a trend can be noticed which reveals one or the other source: with a Protestant writer a particular tendency in the history of ideas may come to the fore; with a Catholic his dependence on prevailing opinions in dogmatic theology may determine and narrow his viewpoint from the outset.

Although we shall have to return to it frequently in the main part of this work, we must say something here about the immediate occasion for its production. In the course of a series of lectures at a German university in the years 1970 to 1971, under the heading of 'Introduction to the New Testament', the teacher tried to give the audience an objective view of Judaism in the period between the Old and New Testaments. The intention was to look at the Jewish literature of that time and to make clear Jewish traditional exegesis, the use of the terms *midrash*, *halachah*, and *haggadah*, the messianic expectations at the time of Jesus from the specifically Jewish standpoint, without slipping into the former method of comparing all this with Christianity to the disparagement of Judaism. On the average the students were in their first to fourth term, their ages ranging from twenty

4

to thirty years. Perhaps it was somewhat risky to assign them as voluntary work, among other things, the theme: 'How do you explain the general lack of understanding of Jesus on the part of his contemporaries?' Certainly the teacher had not expected all the students choosing this theme to treat it negatively. They produced essays which in form were most carefully constructed. The content, however, with exact references to sources and quotations, and the conclusions corresponded not to what they had heard in the generally well-attended lectures, but to the old familiar explanation of Schürer and his successors.[6] The students had done their work thoroughly, they had consulted the abundance of relevant literature at their disposal, by the most diverse authorities, and had made no distinction between Protestant and Catholic writers.

The result of these efforts was so unexpectedly negative as to dismay not only the teacher herself but also the other professors and assistants working in the field of Old or New Testament studies there. It must be stressed at once that there was no question of anti-Semitism in the ordinary sense. None of the students and no member of the teaching body was under any sort of 'handicap'. The causes of the anti-Judaistic treatment of this theme—admittedly a difficult one—lie on another plane which has hitherto been too little investigated. They seem to be the direct consequence of the way in which university professors in general speak and write of Jews and Judaism, when they are describing the origins and early teachings of Christianity. The students' essays are important and revealing inasmuch as they indicate in their bibliographies, notes, and quotations what books are consulted today, what they say about Judaism, and how the average theological student accepts uncritically the information with which he is presented—despite the historical experiences of the last forty years. He seems to be completely unaware of the fact that this material might not be entirely accurate—for him the names of the authors possess an indisputable authority—nor can he appreciate to what extent his reading influences his own attitude for the future. This is all the more disturbing because most of these theology students will by now be active as pastors or teachers of religion, and

5

their inadequate and biased information on Jews and Judaism will thus reach large circles of people who are even less adequately informed.

Therefore, although the investigations of the school material already carried out in different countries are excellent, as long as the teacher himself in the course of his studies receives an inadequate or distorted picture of Judaism, all attempts to produce an objective and sympathetic attitude are involved in a vicious circle. It is notable how little impression the historical events of the last decades have left on university teachers; only in a very few cases have they led to any attempt at a new interpretation of the relationship between the Jewish community and the early Christian Church and to a better understanding of the role of Judaism.

Shortly before this survey was completed, the author received a book which had just appeared, *Judentum im Christlichen Religionsunterricht*, containing these important observations: 'We really cannot complain about the mass of books and review articles on New Testament exegesis which have appeared in the last decades in Germany. . . . But there is one investigation for which I have been looking for a long time, a book on anti-Judaism in the publications of German New Testament scholars from 1945 onwards. The statistical basis alone of this investigation would require much time and effort; but we must ask particularly which of us German theologians is so familiar with Judaism that he could see whenever statements on Judaism and its relationship to Christianity were lacking in objectivity. And, last but not least, which of us would have the courage to write such a book? He could not fail to be afraid of falling between all the theological chairs.'[7] Heinz Kremers, the author of this article, then points out how German students are shocked when they read studies of Judaism by American authors and then see these ignored or reproduced in a distorted form by German scholars. Kremers rightly suggests that the reason for the false presentation of Judaism in the works of most New Testament scholars is that they continue to appeal to the old collections of material and to the conclusions drawn from these, in particular to Strack/Billerbeck.

It seems really necessary therefore to examine the books consulted by theology students today in order to see what is their approach to Judaism. This does not mean that we are going to charge individual authors with anti-Semitism; with many of them the very opposite is the case. But it remains true that what many of them know about the 'nature of Judaism' is only what their predecessors have taught and that—now as before—they start out from the following theses:

1   Judaism has been superseded and replaced by Christianity.

2   Consequently—this is rarely expressed so brutally today —Judaism has scarcely any right to continue to exist.

3   In any case its teaching and ethical values are inferior to those of Christianity.

4   The Christian theologian continues to assume that he has the right to pass judgement on Judaism, its destiny, and its task in the world—or even to be permitted to dictate this task.

5   Only some few real specialists in the departments of Jewish studies make a fresh examination of authentically Jewish sources. In most cases the material collected in certain works about the turn of the century is taken over as a matter of course and quoted, without bothering about the Jewish interpretation of the sources or considering how the Jews see themselves.

6   We often find that the same author when he expressly speaks of Judaism in an ecumenical context has a strikingly different approach from that which he adopts when he is dealing mainly with the Christian religion and mentions Judaism more or less incidentally.

Before making a closer investigation of the relevant material in subsequent chapters, we may cite some brief examples here, each of which throws light on one of the above theses:

1   'In him the history of Israel had come, rather, to its real end. What did belong to the history of Israel was the

process of his rejection and condemnation by the Jerusalem religious community. It had not discerned in him the goal to which the history of Israel had secretly been leading ... Only a few had joined him, and from them something new had proceeded. The Jerusalem religious community ... kept aloof from this new movement. Hereafter the history of Israel moved quickly to its end.'[8]

2 'With the advent of the New Covenant the Old Covenant is outdated. Christian revelation on the other hand is eternally young. But, with its coming, the existence of those who prepared it has lost any real meaning. It is in a sense paradoxical that the Old Testament people of God, despite this obsolescence, should continue to exist simultaneously with the people of the New Testament.'[9]

3 '"*Blessed are the merciful, for they shall obtain mercy.*" The Old Testament form, "He who pursues righteousness and kindness will find life, righteousness and honour" (Proverbs 21.21) sounds too much like late-Jewish legalistic piety, as if God had to grant rewards even in the present life and as if almsgiving could give rise to a more or less legal claim to reward. If Jesus declared the merciful blessed, it was in the "eschatological" sense, a sense familiar to the community.'[10]

4 'Thus, without entering on a mission to the Jews, it becomes at the same time a matter for the Church to draw Judaism's attention to its task, in which it has hitherto failed; to teach it to understand the prophets as the completely final heralds of its task and Jesus as their continuer, calling the individual Jew to a decision.'[11]

5 'Children. Closely connected with the new position which Jesus accords to women in the sphere of the approaching *basileia* is a new view of children. In the world of Jesus, children, like women, were counted as things of little value. Jesus, on the other hand ... promises salvation to children as such ... As a result, he brings children nearer to God than adults.'[12] In a footnote Jeremias cites various legal prescriptions from the Talmud which certainly do

not suggest that children are despised, but only that they need special tutelage. In this respect he is following, among other authorities, the commentary on Mark in the *Regensburger Neues Testament* (Regensburg, 1963, p. 188), but has not properly understood the rabbinic view of children. We may recall the explanation of Rabbi Juda: 'The Sanhedrin were exiled but the Shechinah did not go into exile with them. The priestly watches were exiled but the Shechinah did not go into exile with them. When, however, the little children were exiled, the Shechinah went into exile with them' (Midrash Rabbah on Lamentations 1.6,33).

6 In his masterpiece, *Herrlichkeit*, in the chapter on 'The Ruins of the Old Covenant', Hans Urs von Balthasar says: 'The covenant constantly infringed by the people was one day shattered by the action of God's word, abolished and deemed not again to be restored. Sin surpassed ... any atonement possible to men, the great harlot Jerusalem was burnt with the fire of God's glory and destroyed.'[13] In his book *Who is a Christian?* his approach is very different: 'And in its initial, still hesitant dialogue with the Jews the Church must feel really humble—small, as they say. Why should the Jews bother to listen only to the voice of the Church after everything that has happened over a period of nearly two thousand years? ... Just think how the Church must appear to our Jewish brothers. What is to be done? Perhaps the Church can submit an inclusive admission of guilt, beginning with a great list of its various examples of non–observance of Scripture; that God retains the right to judge others ... At no point is the Church so seriously required to be humble and lowly as in this case. It's not out of place to say that it is asked to realize its shame and disgrace.'[14] It is not easy to harmonize these two statements of the same author. In the first God's judgement on Israel is described as finally accomplished; in the second, much more cautiously, not Israel but the Church's conduct in regard to Israel is condemned.

In the light of these quotations it must be admitted that there
is a danger in the present investigation which cannot always
be avoided: it is almost impossible to do justice to every author
who is quoted. There is not sufficient time or space to give
more than brief excerpts from his work. We can scarcely enter
here into his methodological, philosophical, and cultural
assumptions. In every case—apart perhaps from one exception
to be mentioned shortly—it should be recognized that each
of them has made his inquiries, taught, and written to the best
of his knowledge and belief. But this does not mean that he
can escape the critical questioning of those who regard as binding the words of the Second Vatican Council in Chapter 4 of
the *Declaration on the Relationship of the Church to Non-
Christian Religions* and whose task it is to give expression to
this text in the living practice of the Church. The final version
runs: 'All should take pains, then, lest in catechetical instruction
and in the preaching of God's word they teach anything out
of harmony with the truth of the gospel and the spirit of Christ'
(Abbot translation). In the light of the conclusions of the present
study it is unfortunate that this should have been the final
formulation. For what 'the truth of the gospel' means with
reference to the Jews is still a matter of dispute, and it is not
clear what is the 'spirit of Christ' with which it seems very
disparaging, biased, and condemnatory statements by Christians
about Jews can be made compatible. It would have been clearer
for Christian theology—which has to speak of Christ—if the
penultimate version of this statement had been allowed to stand:
'All should take pains, then, lest in catechetical instruction and
in the preaching of God's word they teach anything which might
rouse hatred or contempt for the Jews in the hearts of the faithful.'[15]

The expressions 'hatred' and 'contempt' are certainly too
strong if applied to the following examples of the exposition
of Christian teaching on Jews and Judaism in the literature on
this subject. The authors deliberately avoid anything of the kind.
But judgements without adequate knowledge of the facts, an
excessive trust in their predecessors in the field of Jewish studies,
disregard, a certain want of empathy such as is often exhibited

today towards other non-Christian religions: enough of all this is found in the authors whose opinions are examined here. And the same tendencies will certainly be roused or strengthened in most of the uncritical readers, just because the writers enjoy such unquestioned authority and because their knowledge in so many fields has rightly earned them a worldwide reputation.

As already mentioned, we shall not deny the good faith of the scholars quoted here or at least their sincere efforts to maintain it, with one exception: those theologians at the time of the Hitler regime who were at pains to detach Christianity from its Jewish roots and to disguise it as 'Aryan'. There is no point here in following up these attempts of pseudo-scholars who came with the Nazi regime and likewise disappeared with it. They belong, at most, to the history of political anti-Semitism. But there are some who either still stand for what they taught in the thirties or whose books went into new editions in the sixties. So in the year 1940 Walter Grundmann produced his *Jesus der Galiläer und das Judentum* in the series *Veröffentlichungen des Instituts zur Erforschung des jüdischen Einflusses auf das deutsche kirchliche Leben*. There he attempts to show that Jesus, being mentally and psychologically completely un-Jewish, must have been the same even biologically and physically. He tries to prove this from the Galilean descent of Jesus through Mary and with the aid of the a late-Jewish legend, which is completely unhistorical and polemical in origin, that he apparently had a non-Jewish father, a Roman soldier called Panthera. The Gospels of the infancy—especially that of Matthew, with his genealogy—are said to have emerged and been circulated in order to discredit these rumours. It is of course true that scarcely anyone today—unless he is interested in this period for other reasons—will take seriously this book or others like it.

On the other hand, however, Grundmann, despite this certainly forgotten book, has remained well known as an author in the field of New Testament studies. In 1965, together with Johannes Leipoldt, he produced a work in three volumes, often quoted and used generally by students: *Die Umwelt des Urchristentums*. We may rightly ask if his approach to the

Jewish background of primitive Christianity is as free from bias as might be expected. In 1961 the third edition appeared of *Die Geschichte Jesu Christi* by the same author. This will be quoted below. Meanwhile we shall merely point out that, although he does not return to the opinions expressed in 1940, Grundmann continues to exaggerate the cultural and religious differences between Jerusalem and Galilee and that on the whole his picture of Judaism has remained one-sided and negative.

Grundmann is not alone in his opinion of the non-Jewish descent of Jesus, nor are those who agree with him only the supporters of the 'German Christians' (whose views are not under consideration here). No less a person than Martin Dibelius agreed with this view already in 1939. His book on Jesus is more important than that of Grundmann, above-mentioned. Firstly, because the author enjoys a worldwide authority as one of the pioneers of the school of Form-Criticism. Secondly, this book went into a new edition in 1960 and in an easily accessible, cheap format in the Göschen Collection. In his introduction the editor, the well-known Marburg theologian, W. G. Kümmel, says that this masterly portrayal has lost nothing of its value with the passing of the years. In this book the Jewish origin of Jesus is seriously questioned, as if it were a disadvantage. Even if Jesus were of David's line, his 'pure Jewish descent is not thereby assured nor a Galilean origin excluded'. He goes on: 'Even if his family ... had settled in Galilee some generations earlier, a doubt as to its purely Jewish character would still be permissible.'[16] An argument of this kind itself leads us to expect in what follows a disparaging attitude to all that is Jewish: an expectation which is also fulfilled.

Gerhard Kittel, who died in 1948, the original editor of the *Theological Dictionary of the New Testament*, an irreplaceable reference book for exegetes and theologians, must also be mentioned here. In 1933 he published his book, *Die Judenfrage*, in which he adopted a very unequivocal attitude to the Jews of his own time and defined them from the Christian standpoint. For him genuinely religious Jews are those alone who are neither liberal nor ritualistic and who 'give an obedient assent to God's history; who in obedience ... take on themselves the suffering of dispersal'.[17] Assimilation and Zionism are both betrayals of Judaism and, however long it may continue, 'authentic Judaism abides by the symbol of the stranger wandering restless and homeless on the face of the earth'.[18]

The attitude of the editor of this important work then made its mark also on his collaborators, so that in a number of the articles in the dictionary—and not only in the volumes which appeared before 1945—it is possible to find traces of a biased or at least scarcely sympathetic approach to Judaism. We shall have to return to this work. Here we may simply add that this idea of 'authentic Judaism' symbolized by 'the stranger wandering restless and homeless on the face of the earth' is not merely of historical or of cultural-political interest for the thirties in Germany. The anti-Zionist view, prevalent today in certain church circles both of the left and of the right, is closely linked with this idea of obedience to God's history with his people of Israel. Here is one of the points at which it becomes evident that theological theory and political behaviour can still be mutually dependent even today.

How little the concrete situation of human relationships is considered finds expression also in the fact that Christian theology in the years 1945 to 1971 speaks of Judaism in the same way as it did before 1945 and even before 1937. This seems to suggest that theologians are scarcely aware of how far their theories, views, and attitudes have influenced and continue to influence Christians in their relations with Jews alive today. It should be stressed once again that the situation is different with books dealing directly with Jewish-Christian relations. These speak in an objective way, sometimes with some exaggeration of guilt and the need of atonement in regard to what is called secular, sociological anti-Semitism, even exhibiting often a kind of not very attractive philosemitism. But in the purely theological-exegetical works Jews and Judaism are discussed now as before as if they formed an abstract something, existing in a vacuum, and not as a living factor in the world today; not as if it were a question of millions of human beings living among us. The authors cited in the following chapters did not consider it necessary to cope with Judaism as a religion and way of life living on after nineteen hundred years, but interpreted *a priori* certain statements of the New Testament as a last word—a word of condemnation.

Here then lies the core of the problem, which can be merely indicated and not solved in the present study. Is the traditional interpretation of the New Testament statements on Judaism the only one possible? Or is the exegetical-theological work of recent years—at least on the continent of Europe—suffering from the absence of a theology of Israel? Such a theology would not annul the binding force of the New Testament for Christians, but it would enable us so to interpret the New Testament that Israel and Judaism would no longer be considered merely as a pedagogue, as preparing the way for Christianity, but as a way of faith which remains valid and is meant to continue developing dynamically alongside the Christian way; for in it the Spirit of God is at work, even in the Christian era. All that we know today of the Judaism of the last two thousand years points to the fact that it continues to play a positive role in the world, that it is not an anachronistic survival from a past epoch. The Church emerged from it; but, together with and despite the existence of the Church, Judaism has not ceased to exist.[19]

The author of this book would admit that it might have been possible—perhaps even necessary—to comment in greater detail on the statements quoted. She is aware that this—and certainly also the hastily drawn conclusions—will expose her work to the criticism of some theologians. But a beginning had to be made somewhere. The book might be described as a pilot project, a pioneer work intended to stimulate further studies, probing more deeply and offering answers to the charges made here. If it has merely succeeded in provoking a discussion leading to further publications on the themes mentioned here, despite all its possible defects, the work will have been worth while.

2
'Late Judaism' and 'Jewish Religious Community'

The method applied in the following survey seemed to emerge spontaneously: it is both thematic and chronological. The themes are those most frequently treated by the authors and in which the centuries-old, biased attitude is most clearly expressed. They are also the very themes with which each and everyone who studies the early Christian period must necessarily cope. The chronological method has the advantage of showing how much the modern author remains dependent on his predecessors and how he takes over their quotations from the Jewish sources together with the conclusions drawn from these, usually without submitting them to a new and objective scrutiny. Contemporary writers are of the greatest importance for this investigation, since it always seemed possible that they might have made a new attempt to find an exegesis more just and more sympathetic to Judaism. The chronological survey begins each time with more recent books and then works backwards to their predecessors. In this way we can see how far the modern scholar remains dependent on his teachers and relies on their opinions and conclusions.

This chapter deals with the theme which also comes chronologically and logically first with the authors quoted: a theme which gave them the necessary scope for the portrayal of Judaism in the period between the two Testaments (occasionally extended backwards to the Babylonian exile and forwards to the revolt of bar Kokhba). The very terminology adopted makes this historical background appear from the outset in the worst light.

What is common to the authors cited here is their view of

15

Jewish religion after the Exile. They see this as a break with the true Yahweh-faith of ancient Israel. Something new emerged, a kind of ethical world-view which can scarcely be called religion any longer. The former religion, founded on trust and love for the God who had rescued the Israelites from bondage and made them his covenant-people was forgotten, and a progressive decline set in, leading away from Israel to Judaism.

Georg Fohrer (who is—among other things—editor of the *Beihefte zur Wissenschaft des Alten Testaments*) gives the following explanation: 'In fact he [Ezra] created early Judaism and laid its religious foundations in the Pentateuch. He ascribed equal importance to ethical and ritual conduct. . . . Ezra's reform finally set the mainstream of Yahwism on the course that turned its back on the insights and principles that had previously prevailed, above all on the message of the prophets. Here we are dealing with more than a reshaping of Israelite Yahwism—a new religion was in the making.'[1] Only in the book of Job do we find an exception, an anticipation of the 'Christian' trust in God as opposed to the new 'Judaistic' system and its 'rationalistic calculation with which the [post-Exilic] doctrine of retribution answers the question of the riddle of existence and the meaning of suffering . . . He [Job] decides to renounce comfortable tradition and safe calculation, breaking through into new and unexplored territory.'[2] Only in the book of Job do we find the genuinely prophetic faith.

For Judaism in general, however, there is a break with the tradition of the past; after the Exile the prophetic message is no longer understood and consequently Israel moves on to the wrong track. It is at this point that the development from the Israelitic religion to 'Judaism' sets in. The fact that the prophets had 'surmounted the approach of religious nationalism' was forgotten or misunderstood. 'For the God they preached refuses to place himself at the disposal of a people or nation, and is not the guarantor of national power or culture.'[3] According to the author, 'Judaism' has thus abandoned the true faith proclaimed by the prophets and replaced it after the Exile with ritualistic and legalistic piety.

In his *Studien zur alttestamentlichen Theologie und Geschichte*, which appeared in the same year, Fohrer defended even more insistently his view of the opposition between the prophetic faith of 'Israel' and the rejection of this very faith by 'Judaism'. 'In face of this God [of the prophetic proclamation] all cult was bound to break down and come to an end.'[4] What is known as 'Judaism' or—in the following centuries—'late Judaism' is based on this cult. This is where it went wrong, for 'priesthood and temple are ripe for destruction ... The whole business of cult in the last resort only leads to sin, in fact the cult itself is already basically sin.'[5]

How does Fohrer reach this conclusion? The Jewish people —no longer God's chosen Israel—thinks it has accomplished by its cult all it owes to God and thus that it has a free hand in ordinary life to follow its own peevish will. 'It does not permit God to be the power determining life and no longer takes his moral requirements seriously.'[6]

It seems difficult to reconcile what has just been said with the wisdom literature of the time and with all that we know of the development and interiorization of Jewish biblical interpretation and liturgical piety in those years. Both biblical writers and teachers of the law, without exception, attached the greatest importance to interior obedience, which however must find concrete expression in fulfilling all the demands even of ordinary life. Israel rightly never thought much of a purely inward religion. But Fohrer goes further in his criticism of Judaism's apostasy from God: it was Israel's task 'to lead its life, not by its own will and for its own purposes, but as an example of a life formed by God's will ... Thus Israel and Judaism as its successor have failed in their divine task by constantly falling away from the way of life imposed on them and wanting to use God merely as metaphysical security for their own life.'[7]

For Fohrer there is a logical connection between the false track of post-Exilic Judaism, which misunderstood its divine mandate, and all the later disasters and persecutions which came upon it, even in the modern European countries. 'For it certainly cannot be overlooked that all this was provoked largely by the misuse of powers lying in Jewish hands—a misuse which again has its cause in the ancient abandonment of Israel's task and in its typically human quest for enjoyment and security of life.'[8] What is here described as 'typically human' therefore is not permitted to the Jews; it does not fit in with the form of life and the task which the author prescribes for the Jewish people.

What began in the centuries after the Exile continued to develop logically up to modern times: Judaism sees itself as a religion, not as a people, but it produces nothing new in the nineteenth-century efforts for reform. 'It was purely and simply the denial of what is properly Jewish for the sake of political-legal security and therefore the denial of the task of Judaism. If in the past it had misunderstood its task and failed in it, it was now no longer aware of the task.'[9] From these quotations it is clear that the author regards Zionism and the Israeli state as evidence merely of a further failure on the part of Israel. But more of this later.

Very similar ideas are expressed in two lectures by Hans Werner Bartsch in Frankfurt in 1970. There he explains why the Bible is 'more widely read than ever' in the state of Israel even by Jews who 'claim to be liberal-rationalists or atheists'.[10] 'In order to understand this, we must realize that Israel's religion was never a religion in the strict sense either in antiquity or today.'[11] Israel's faith is not a religion, but historical reflection. What is really decisive for this historical awareness is 'the exodus from the house of slavery in Egypt to the freedom of nomadic existence up to the settlement in the promised land of Canaan. Subsequent history . . . is then judged by the extent to which that freedom which Israel experienced as characteristic of its own existence in the forty years in the desert was maintained and proved in the country. The destruction of their own state in 587 B.C. [and the subsequent exile] are regarded as the consequence of failing to preserve freedom in their own people.'[12] This seems to be a very arbitrary judgement on religious-historical events with which we are familiar. In the first place the exodus from Egypt is intelligible only as part of a greater event, namely the Sinai covenant of God with his people, with a view to taking possession of the promised land.

Secondly, the liberation or non-liberation of the Jewish slaves is only one of the causes and not the main one for the exile in the sixth century. It is mentioned only once, in Jeremiah 34.8–17.

For Bartsch anyway this one-sided and highly original emphasis is necessary in order to prove his thesis, that the essential thing for Israel was not the settled condition of the nation in a particular country but the fulfilment of a special ideal for which settlement in a country of their own is not necessary. Israel's task is to realize an ethical idea: 'Jerusalem acquired a kind of symbolic value for a social order which, in contrast to the existing slave-owning society, provided freedom for everyone.'[13] This thesis seems so much more arbitrary in the light of the fact that both in Palestine and in the Diaspora Jews completely accepted ownership of slaves as an obvious necessity for agriculture, even though their laws—the Sabbath precept, provisions for the Year of Jubilee—constantly demanded the humane treatment of slaves and even their eventual liberation. Nevertheless he continues to elaborate his thesis: 'Essentially therefore the significance of Jerusalem is not religious in character.'[14]

It is Bartsch's thesis that the bond of the Jews to the country of Israel and in particular to the city of Jerusalem has nothing to do with religion. This for him is of the greatest importance, since he wants to prove that the foundation of the state is opposed to the proper task of Jews in the world. He regards it as his own task to make them aware again of their real mission. If Israel will renounce possession of this city then 'the city of Jerusalem will win back the significance it has beyond all nationalistic strivings. It will become the expression of the longing for freedom with which the Jewish people in the ghettos were filled.'[15] Their time as nomads in the desert and their stay in the ghettos are here regarded as the ideal state of affairs, since at that time their longing for freedom could be most clearly expressed. It is only on condition of not being tied to a country or a city that Israel can fulfil its real task, which it has neglected from the time of the Babylonian exile: to be free from any nationalistic tie and to give a living example of this

19

ideal in the midst of other nations. If we think of the last two thousand years of Jewish existence among the nations, we may be inclined to charge Bartsch with unconscious cynicism; for Jewish history in these twenty centuries is anything but an example of life lived in freedom.

For Werner Förster also, from the sixth century before Christ, 'the lack of national independence is not only an historic fact of Judaism but, at the same time, one of its essential features'.[16] The prophets had predicted this and therefore the greater part of those deported also understood the Diaspora as the existence destined by God for his people. It may be mentioned merely incidentally that this is false in both historical and religious terms, for it was precisely the élite of the exiles who returned at different times to that country where alone it was possible to serve God perfectly in accordance with his will: their first work was the reconstruction of the temple. But to return to Förster's understanding of the situation: 'Ever since the Babylonian captivity Judaism has been "on the move", on the move between judgement and grace. "Judaism" is therefore comprised of the children of Israel, who know themselves to be on the move, driven from normal independent existence as a people, driven from the land of their fathers because of their sins, on the move towards a time of salvation, which God himself will bring to pass, when he will ... turn the captivity of Israel, on the move under the cloud of God's judgement and God's grace. Life in exile is thus an essential feature of Judaism.'[17]

According to this view, the re-emergence of a state as a result of Cyrus' decree in the sixth century before Christ was a misunderstanding of God's will for Israel, a blunder which was bound to lead to a wrong conception of its religion in subsequent centuries and which ended in the disaster of the year A.D. 70. If 'life in exile' is in fact an 'essential feature' of Judaism, then the founding of the state in 1948 is merely a repetition of the revolt against God's dispensation two thousand five hundred years ago, against the Diaspora existence imposed on Israel by God. It is from this source that all the mistakes have arisen since then in the understanding of their own faith and in regard to their proper task: 'The belief, inspired by the Old Testament,

20

that God chose Israel out of an unconditional love is overlaid and rendered ineffective by the other view that Israel was chosen because it *is* better than the other nations.'[18] The author can cite no proof from Jewish sources that this view of its election prevails today or that it ever prevailed. On the contrary, this election was understood always as a task and never as a preference or a privilege liberating the people from their duties.

Martin Metzger's book is particularly important since it is meant to provide the student with a brief, easily assimilated introduction to the history of Israel right up to New Testament times. But it can more easily lead to prejudices since it attempts to be as concise as possible and cites only some few examples which the author regards as typical, but which in fact are only marginally relevant to Jewish religious teaching—something that the student himself of course cannot control. Thus it is said that 'rabbinic biblical scholarship reached its peak in the first century'. And the examples of this 'peak': 'Every possible case was discussed and the attempt was made to deduce binding rules for all spheres of life. Was it permissible to eat an egg laid by a hen on the Sabbath? Was it permissible to rescue a donkey which had fallen into a well on the Sabbath?[19] If just these examples are presented as the 'peak' of rabbinical interpretation of the Bible, it is not surprising that the Christian reader finds this allegedly 'classical' interpretation—described without reference to the deep respect for God's word and his moral requirements which lies behind it—the product of a decadent scholarship, preoccupied with the letter of the Bible and as such exaggerated and absurd, typical of 'late Judaism'.

It must also be pointed out that Metzger, like Fohrer, Bartsch, and many others, speaks not of a Jewish *people* in its own country, but of a 'Jewish religious community'.[20] This is a subtle way of arriving at an *a priori* approach which separates nation, religion, and country of Israel from one another. A 'religious community' assembles for certain rites and a liturgy; it is not tied to a nation or a country. The use of the term 'religious community' serves precisely to suggest that Israel, which had been moulded into a nation during ten to twelve centuries through and after the settlement in the promised land, was established after the Exile merely as a religious community centred on the temple and linked together by the cultic 'law'. The concept of the existence of a 'religious community', which ceased to be a people in late Judaism, has had a political influence up to very recent times; for a 'religious community' as such has no title to a country, nor can the possession of a state have any particular meaning or purpose for it. A religious community is not a people, but only a fellowship of believers united by a common faith. Hence today also the anti-Zionist attitude of many theologians, which arises precisely from this false conception of Jewish life after the Exile.

Günther Schiwy's popular introductions appearing in cheap editions are widely read by students. For him late Judaism is only a preparation for Christianity and much inferior to the latter in its religious ideas. So (like others) he speaks, for example, of the use of 'Father' as a form of address for God, a form frequently used in the period between the Testaments. 'In this Hebraic *ab* . . . the religious consciousness of Judaism does in fact rise to addressing God as "Father" in order to remind him of his promises, but this is not yet the intimate-sounding *abba* of Aramaic conversational language, expressing the individual's personal affection and feeling of security, with which Jesus begins his prayers and which gives this Our Father its own, new resonance.'[21] Thus expressions common to Jews and later to Christians are compared and their value depreciated when used by Jews—without any good reason—merely in order to prove the superiority of the new religious community; as if it would have been detrimental to Christianity simply to adopt the form of address—'Father'—long familiar in Jewish prayer language and expressive of trust in him who is after all the same God.

In the very useful three-volume work edited by J. Leipoldt and W. Grundmann the rich depths of Jewish religion at that time are recognized, since the authors have studied late Judaism more thoroughly and portrayed it more adequately than the last two above-mentioned. These admissions, however, are made somewhat reluctantly and positive statements are usually accompanied by negative restrictions, as in the following with reference to prayer: 'Faith in the God who directs the history of his people and has his eye on each individual is expressed in a truly splendid way in such a shaping and conduct of life'; but the sentence continues, 'a splendour which cannot be obscured by the danger of exteriorization and the display of pious craving for fame and righteousness of works'.[22] Unfortunately the terminology itself already obscures this splendour.

Eduard Lohse, who really knows the Judaism of the period between the two Testaments and later, goes a step further and denies even the 'religious community' its title to the temple itself: 'Through the temple, Israel's holy place, the community of the disciples [of Jesus] is united with the people of God of the Old Testament. This [the temple] is no longer the legitimate possession of the Jews, but the place where Jesus' disciples—who have experienced the fulfilment of the Old Testament promises—make the praises of God ring out. The turning from the old to the new is accomplished in fact in the history of Jesus. Together with his disciples, he makes the temple again the centre of right worship of God.'[23] This creates the impression that the temple had hitherto been the centre of a wrong, erroneous worship of God which had taken place in late Judaism and was only now being corrected.

Some will be pained to find so great a spiritual writer as Romano Guardini quoted here: a man who, in the course of his long literary career, helped many people to find a hearing in their quest for the meaning of life. But, as far as 'late Judaism' is concerned, he belongs wholly to the tradition described here. This is how he sees the situation after the Exile and the wars of the Maccabees: 'The voices of the prophets are silenced. From the worldly viewpoint, the representatives of the Law have won [note the contrast so often found between prophetic message and 'law']. They have succeeded in reducing God and his will to a guarantor of the glory of human law. The lower the nation's outer power sank, the prouder, more fanatical grew the hopes of the law-makers ... Thus the covenant founded on faith and grace, that wonderful exchange of loyalty for loyalty, of trust for divine aid, became a documented charter of rights and demands.'[24] This was *the* great error of late Judaism which will

23

be considered at greater length in the chapter on 'Law'. In another passage Guardini quite rightly sees that 'Israel's history had been shaped by its faith in God.'[25] Through this faith it could hold its own against the surrounding world-powers and their civilization for a thousand years. 'Secure in its monotheistic belief, it had been able to overcome the spiritual and religious forces around it. However, in this belief in the one-and-only God, it had also begun to grow harsh and rigid.'[26] This is the supreme charge which is constantly levelled in one form or another against post-Exilic Judaism, which in fact brands religious Judaism as 'late Judaism': 'grown harsh and rigid' in its faith. The fact that, on the contrary, incisive and deeply religious developments took place among the people from the time of the Exile and of Ezra—the emergence of the synagogues, of times of prayer even far away from the temple, the ideas of penance and atonement, which stem from these centuries—all this is ignored by these authors or regarded as false, rigid, legalistic piety.

Of all the biblical scholars here mentioned Martin Noth may be regarded as one of the best known and most widely read. He it is also who regards the national life of Israel and even its mere existence as definitively ended after the Exile or at the latest after the year A.D. 70. He says nothing at all to explain who are the Jews who—despite this 'end'—have survived the last two thousand years with their own political, cultural, and religious life. According to him, the confederacy of the twelve tribes ceased in 587 B.C. and so too the covenant and the legal system which belonged only to this institution. Oddly enough, however, he does not mention the fact that in the year 587 there were no longer twelve tribes, but only two, while the other ten had ceased from the eighth century B.C. even to be a schismatic part of the Israelitic nation. This end of Israel as a whole had already been announced by the prophets. They had explained the coming historical disasters which were to break over Israel as '. . . God's judgement on the people of Israel. This judgement would mark the end of the old relationship between God and people . . . Since the people of Israel had not maintained the loyalty required by the establishment of the covenant, nor

upheld the exclusive worship of one single God with all its consequences, therefore the announcement of the covenant relationship which had accompanied its establishment would now find
its divine repudiation in large-scale historical catastrophes, and
at the same time the covenant would from now on be cancelled
by God.'[27] History itself proves that God had prepared the
end of the Old Covenant.

'For these people their own times [the centuries between the
Babylonian exile and the year A.D. 70] had the character of a
dwindling period of transition; the actual end of the old order
was not regarded as final and decisive ... Consequently, in
theory and in practice, the validity of the old law was allowed
to stand ... This certainly meant that the declarations of classical
prophecy, interpreting what had happened as a sealing of the
end of the covenant between God and people, were not accepted
in full earnestness or with complete finality.'[28] Noth does in
fact mention the covenant renewal under Ezra, which was
regarded as a legitimate continuation of the existing and never
completely dissolved covenantal relationship, but adds that this
was a mistake: 'The real crux, the question of the connection
between all this and God, is not seriously considered.'[29]
Certainly there is talk of transgression and sin, but it was never
assumed that 'the great historical catastrophes ... had in fact
brought that ancient Israel to an end'.[30] Israel does not understand its own fall. Holding on to the covenant is one-sided and
wilful obstinacy; in reality 'covenant' is replaced by 'law'.

How is it possible for so great an expert on the Old Testament
so to misjudge the prophetic promises of a Deutero-Isaiah, of
a Jeremiah, the Books of Ezra and Nehemiah, as also the post-
Exilic consoling words in Deuteronomy about God's unshakable
fidelity to the covenant with his people despite their sins? This
can be understood only if we assume that he regards all these
promises no longer as directed to the historical Israel and that
he is mainly interested in seeing all events as oriented to the
'New Covenant', in applying them in a spiritual sense to Christianity.

In his *History of Israel* Noth speaks even more clearly. It
is he also who consistently describes post-Exilic Israel merely

as a 'religious community'. For, with the Diaspora in the sixth century, which becomes definitive in the first century, 'Israel ceased to exist and the history of Israel came to an end'.[31] With the revolt of bar Kokhba 'a sequel did in fact take place ... and this sequel therefore forms an appendix to the history of Israel, which had really already come to an end'.[32] He calls this heroic episode of Jewish history 'a slow and agonizing death in which the newly revived "Israel" perished'.[33] And 'so the descendants of the Israel of old had become strangers in their former homeland just as they were in the Diaspora; and their holy city was prohibited to them. Thus ended the ghastly epilogue of Israel's history.'[34]

There is another aspect, however, of this 'ghastly epilogue', which does not make the author's *a priori* standpoint correct but at least explains it, for the following lines show clearly how Noth considers the whole history of Israel from a thoroughly Christian standpoint. It reaches its culmination and end in the advent of Jesus: 'Jesus himself, with his words and his work, no longer formed part of the history of Israel. In him the history of Israel had come, rather, to its real end. What did belong to the history of Israel was the process of his rejection and condemnation by the Jerusalem religious community. It had not discerned in him the goal to which the history of Israel had secretly been leading; it rejected him as the promised Messiah. Only a few had joined him, and from them something new proceeded. The Jerusalem religious community imagined it had more important concerns, and kept aloof from this new movement. Hereafter the history of Israel moved quickly to its end.'[35]

It remains however fundamentally inexplicable how Martin Noth, who also knew the Judaism of later centuries (he himself died in 1969 in Israel and was buried there), could fail to see that this history not only did not come to an end in the year A.D. 70 with the partly political expulsion from Palestine, but continued to develop in harmony with its biblical and post-biblical past; that in subsequent centuries again and again, even under the most difficult political conditions, there were periods when the religious and cultural life of Judaism and the life of the Jews as a nation among the nations reached great heights. The fact that, after the destruction of a third of the Jewish population in the heart of Europe in the present century, Israel still had the strength to re-establish a state of its own is certainly the most impressive proof that 'the history of Israel' in the year A.D. 70 or 135 did not move 'quickly to its end'.

Scarcely any other biblical scholar can have had so permanent an influence on the understanding of the New Testament as Rudolf Bultmann, the co-founder with Martin Dibelius of the school of Form-Criticism. Although it is frequently recognized today that his view of the Old Testament and of Judaism is one-sided and often false, his works continue to enjoy a unique authority. For him too there was no longer a Jewish people even in the period between the two Testaments. 'Can we', he asks, 'seriously designate the Jewish "Church" ['Church', like 'religious community', excludes the idea of 'nation'] of the Persian and Roman era as the realization of the people of God? On the one hand it is a community which is held together and molded not by the forces and forms of a national life, but by the laws of a theoretically conceived *cultus* and ritual, which more and more loses its significance for real life.'[36] In his epoch-making *Theology of the New Testament* he expresses the same opinion that a Jewish people properly speaking did not exist: 'He [Jesus] does not, as the prophets did, raise the demand for justice and right; for the preaching of these things, once decisive for Israelitic national life, has lost its meaning now that there is scarcely any national life left.'[37] It would be interesting to ask in what a truly national life consists. When in the late forties, for instance, Germany was occupied by the Allies and had lost its political autonomy, was there no truly 'national life'?

The religion of Judaism deteriorated also at this time: 'In Judaism God is de-historized by having become a distant God enthroned in heaven; his governance of the world is carried out by angels, and His relation to man is mediated by the book of the Law. And man in Judaism is de-historized by being marked off from the world by ritual and by finding his security within the ritually pure congregation.'[38]

Bultmann can have learned this only from the apocalyptic

27

and Gnostic writings which were alien to normative Judaism; that God is a distant God and that the world is ruled by angels—these are completely un-Jewish ideas which we shall find again in the book by Bousset and Gressmann, which derives its ideas of Judaism almost solely from apocalyptic writings. Bultmann knows little or nothing about the properly Jewish sources of that time as they were later reproduced in the Talmud and Midrash. In Christ's time, when the Jewish liturgy was created in its basic features, God is certainly not 'a distant God'; but, particularly in post-Exilic piety, he becomes as never before a God who is close, while serving him in prayer and daily life penetrates and characterizes all forms of human action. He is present everywhere and in everything far more than it was imagined before the Babylonian exile. Bultmann's main interest lies in working out the contrast between the Christian God brought close to us in Jesus and the Jewish God enthroned in the distance. For the sake of this thesis he gives an arbitrary explanation of the Jewish way of faith and interprets the sources —as far as he knows them at all—in such a manner that they harmonize with his preconceived ideas.

Walter Grundmann adopts the same line. While the prophets stood for the unity between God's will and our relations with our fellow men, even in ancient Israel 'an intrinsic unity between man's relationship to God and his relationship to other men' was never achieved.[39] It is obvious then that 'Judaism', always regarded as a degeneration of 'ancient Israel', has even less appreciation of this view that faith in God and fellowship with men are not to be separated from each other. Grundmann sticks to his opinion, even though he is certainly aware of the famous dictum of Hillel to a pagan who wanted to know what was the essence of Judaism: 'What you don't like yourself, don't do to anyone else' (cf. Tobit 4.15), a saying which is almost literally adopted by Jesus in Matthew 7.12. Grundmann wants to work out the thesis that the call for brotherliness first came from Jesus, while Judaism was merely the 'harsh, joyless service'[40] of a strict God.

It is tedious to find the same ideas expressed again and again in almost the same way. But we must bear with the repetition, since we are here trying to describe the history of an uninterrupted Christian tradition. Martin Dibelius' *Jesus* is a book much used by students. Here too we read of post-Babylonian decadence, the descent from 'Israel' to 'Judaism'. 'This conception of God, very unphilosophical but directly affecting mankind, had of course been enormously narrowed in the theology of Judaism in the centuries between Alexander the Great and the advent of Jesus. The Lord of all peoples had become the party leader of the legalists ... The nation no longer stood in the midst of its own self-determined history, and therefore no longer had any ear for the Lord who acts through nations and upon nations.'[41]

The book first appeared in German in 1939. We can scarcely be wrong therefore in finding here again a number of National Socialist ideas and even expressions ('party leader'). Dibelius returns to the Jewish people's failure to act historically: 'The great world, and indeed the political and social life of their own people with their tasks and problems, vanish from the sight of those who thus confine themselves to the study of the Law and to its application to the minutest sphere of human activity.'[42] How does he explain the great political events of the years A.D. 66–73, 132–5, in which the most devout members of the Jewish people took part? Did those heroic, militant revolts display a lack of interest in history, in the independent existence of the nation? Ought they not to have made an impression particularly on a German theologian at that time?

If the authors listed here were not outstanding scholars every one of whom has made his own contribution to the different branches of Bible study, we should be tempted to charge them with plagiarism, so closely do their opinions and even their forms of expression resemble one another when they come to speak about late Judaism. One of these is Günther Bornkamm, the well-known disciple of Bultmann, who however has gone his own way in the study of the historical Jesus. In his famous *Jesus of Nazareth* he speaks of Judaism: 'Without a doubt the religion of ancient Israel underwent in Judaism after the Exile a tremendous narrowing down and hardening.'[43] He quotes Dibelius to the effect that God had become a 'party leader'.

Israel has sunk to Judaism; it lives—so to speak—archaically, in the past and in the experience of the future, without any valid, independent existence in the present—that is, in the time of Jesus. 'The time during which this expectation of the final consummation took clearer shape is the time of the Exile and the subsequent centuries up to Israel's historical end.'[44] As with Noth and others, it is mentioned more or less incidentally that the Jewish people ceased to exist in the year A.D. 70.

The work of Leonhard Goppelt, devoted particularly to the study of the religious history and the situation of Judaism in the first century, is of the greatest importance. He compares Judaism's rise with that of the Catholic Church: 'In both cases, a people of God traced their origins back to the mighty works of God. But in preserving the record of that origin both of these communities employed certain principles that were not altogether consistent with the original tradition. In adhering to these distinctive principles of interpretation, both communities sought to secure their own places in history',[45] although in both cases they neither rightly understand nor faithfully followed the traditions they wanted to preserve. As far as late Judaism is concerned, it 'as well as the term Jew came into being during and after the *Babylonian Exile* (587–538 B.C.). There would have been no Judaism had there not first been this loss of national self-government and the subsequent scattered existence of the Jewish people in the *Diaspora* (dispersion). The *Diaspora* has, indeed, remained the hallmark of the Jewish people to this day.'[46] It is true that this 'Judaism' was influenced also by the prophetic message, but only superficially. Judaism basically is opposed to prophecy: the former emerges only at the point where 'this hope of salvation was combined with the idea of obedience to the Law'.[47] As proof of this the author (evidently only in the German edition of his book) quotes Romans 4.13, Paul's well-known theology of grace versus law. Consequently, his argument would seem to be patently *a priori*, with no examination of Judaism's own understanding of itself or its own testimonies. So here too 'The community around Jerusalem was never actually the homeland of any considerable part of the Jewish nation ... but for all Jews everywhere it was the home of their hearts, because the Temple was there.'[48] Consequently, with the loss of the temple, the last tie with the homeland is broken and the Jews as a people have ceased to exist. But, when the Jewish people nevertheless acts as a nation and decides to intervene to shape its own history, as in the war against the Seleucids, the author qualifies his position in this way: 'Men can accomplish by force of arms objectives which cannot be attained by patient waiting for the grace of God.'[49] Thus 'the orientation to faith and grace'[50] is removed. The contradiction is obvious. Post-Exilic Judaism is 'unhistorical', but if it acts as a nation and intervenes in history this merely shows its lack of trust in God; whatever it does, it is wrong. Jesus alone gets to the heart of the revelation attested by Scripture in direct opposition to 'a Judaism which had usurped the Old Testament revelation'.[51] Under any circumstances, the comparison between the early Christian and the 'late Jewish' community must turn out to the disadvantage of the latter.

The parable of the wicked wine-growers announces 'that what the prophets had threatened was now taking place in redemptive history, namely, the covenant people as such were being rejected.'[52] He continues. ' "Your house", the Temple or the common life of Israel [why should the Temple alone be the 'common life' of Israel?], would be forsaken by God. It would no longer be His house. The destruction of the Temple which Jesus envisioned in connection with this was simply an expression of this *removal of God's gracious presence*.'[53] And so at the end of his book Goppelt draws the conclusion: 'In fact the rejection of the gospel by Israel as a national community is the last decisive turning point in its history.'[54]

From now on there are two forms of Judaism: 'Old Testament Judaism—existence under the law, encircled by promise—and post-Christian Judaism'[55] which is established by wilful self-assertion. Consequently a distinction must be made between the legitimate Judaism of the Old Testament and 'the late Jewish estate, of which all that survives is what the Lord has thoroughly purified',[56] and this has become the heritage of the Church.

In his eight-volume Catholic dogmatic theology Michael

31

Schmaus asserts that for Israel 'from now on' there remains 'only the opportunity either of deciding to live as an oppressed nation or of opting for Barabbas as the type of political agitator'.[57] For the 'superficial observer', Israel seems 'obsolete and its existence meaningless';[58] nevertheless it still has the eschatological hope of redemption one day by Christ.

Although Ethelbert Stauffer is attacked by some of his colleagues for reasons which have nothing to do with Judaism, his *New Testament Theology* continues to be widely read and circulated. In this work he observes that Jerusalem 'has said "yes", an autocratic, demonic "yes", to the tradition of those who murdered the prophets. Zion became the mountain of the enemies of the Lord.'[59]

Even for so learned and sympathetic an expert on Judaism as Werner Georg Kümmel, the Marburg theologian, late Judaism is an aberration by comparison with the Israel of the Old Testament. It is true that Judaism does not serve a God other than the God of Israel, but the fact is 'that, for the piety of late Judaism, the God active at the present time was concealed by the memory of his gracious action in the past and by the hope of the expectation of salvation in the future'.[60] This is an odd argument. Is not God always present through the memory of his gracious acts in the past? Does not the Christian Eucharist itself rouse and strengthen our present trust in God by recalling the past and by the hope of what he will do in the future? Why then should memory and hope in the future be 'empty of salvation' for Judaism? It is claimed that, if Jesus did not produce any new concept of God, he certainly made known a new *'reality'* of God'[61] which did not and does not exist in Judaism. The question again must be raised as to how the Jewish present—at that time and since then—could be 'empty of salvation', if a whole nation was ready to die for its faith and its existence and never to give up its relationship to God, its 'salvation'.

Finally we must hear those authors who could be described as the past masters of all those cited up to now. In the present survey it is impossible to confine ourselves to the writers of the last twenty to thirty years, since the original attitudes and

32

statements in regard to Judaism in the time of Jesus stem from those who dealt with the subject in the first quarter of the twentieth century and are still regarded as authoritative. It would indeed be possible to go right back to the Church Fathers, but this would go beyond the scope of this work. The men considered here are Bousset/Gressmann, Eduard Meyer, and Emil Schürer. In their work we find the source of all the assertions quoted up to now, so that we can scarcely be surprised to find them adopted as authoritative by all their successors in university departments of theology.

Bousset and Gressmann argue—as many later were to argue —that Israel ceased to exist as a nation in the sixth century B.C. After the Exile there is a break with national and political elements. Judaism becomes 'Church', that is, 'temple community'. Nor can we speak of a real national life even at the time of the Maccabees, but at most of a juxtaposition of 'ecclesiastical' and 'national' trends. Finally, after the bar Kokhba war, 'all that remained in existence was the structure of the rigid Jewish religious community, without any sort of external national background'.[62] The work is not entirely consistent, at least in its terminology, for quite suddenly the term 'nation' is used again: 'In the wild struggles [A.D. 70 and 135] . . . Judaism here too developed completely into the nation hating all and being hated by all, as Tacitus already describes it.'[63] This is a typical example of the failure of the author to consult Jewish sources and of his use of pagan and Christian writings. It would be equally fair to judge Christians by what the pagan writers of the first three centuries said about them: this too would be neither flattering nor truthful. Although Bousset and Gressmann deny Judaism's existence as a 'nation', they continue to use the expression when it suits their purpose: 'In bitter resentment Judaism withdrew from the world, a nation which could neither live nor die, a Church which did not break away from national life and therefore remained a sect.'[64] This is both illogical and untrue. Firstly, if Judaism did not break away from national life, how does it follow that it remained a 'sect'? Secondly, both Jewish and non-Jewish sources prove that Judaism in the first three to four centuries A.D. by no means withdrew from the world; with its centre in Jabneh it lived an extraordinarily intense religious-national life in Palestine, and the President of the Jabneh Sanhedrin was recognized and respected even by the Roman authorities as head of all the Jews living within the Empire. Moreover, Jewish communities lived in many Roman cities and in Babylon and shared—as far as their religion permitted—in the culture of these centres and in their social life. Their religion continued to exercise a great attraction on the pagan population and even—after Constantine —on certain Christian circles. This was one cause of the conflict with the Christian Church.

In another connection—we are talking here about the situation in Judea and Galilee before A.D. 70—Jews are again charged with attaching too much importance to religious life and neglecting their duties in the 'organized life of the community'. They were too much interested in the 'supernatural': 'Secular concern for the welfare of the community they left to the princes and the aristocracy. The devout became traitors to their princes, their catechism says nothing about national duties.'[65] It seems that a Prussian situation—absolute obedience to the prince—is being transferred to the Judaism of the time of Jesus and shortly before it. It was not merely for religious reasons that the later Hasmonean kings and Herod as also the Roman procurators after them were very unpopular with the people. Anyone familiar with Jewish history in those years must know that these rulers were bloody tyrants and that they destroyed whole groups of the population without reason, if the latter seemed to present a threat to their power. Without going into details, we need only refer to Flavius Josephus, who has quite sufficient to say about the many cruel deeds of the rulers at that time. The 'devout' were not at all 'traitors' to their princes, but rightly blamed the princes' unwarranted, arbitrary interventions in the national and religious life of the people.

Bousset and Gressmann seem also to ignore the fact that it is difficult in Judaism to separate the national from the religious element and that no ruler could expect obedience from the Jewish people as a whole if he offended or completely disregarded their religious customs. Apparently Bousset and Gressmann have in mind here a typically German ideal of strict discipline and morality, according to which the subject owes absolute obedience to his ruler: an ideal which led in the sixteenth century to the principle, *cujus regio ejus religio* ('the religion of the country will be that of its ruler'), which any Jew would rightly find completely unintelligible. Hence those times of Jewish resistance are constantly described as 'confused' and 'disorderly'. We shall have to speak later of this failure to understand the genuinely Jewish nature. Here we need only quote finally the opinion of Bousset and Gressman that 'the basic character of late hellenistic Judaism is completely imitative and uncreative'.[66] Evidently the authors are unaware of the almost revolutionary renewal precisely of this Judaism through the Pharisaic interpretation of the biblical religion.

Eduard Meyer takes the same line as Bousset and Gressmann. Since he will be quoted in other connections, it will be sufficient here to mention his approach to a theme we have already frequently encountered: the form of addressing God as Father. Meyer adduces a new and odd-sounding argument: if God is addressed in this way in late Judaism 'this merely means that only the chosen devout ones form the true Israel'.[67] There was only a single group in Judaism, of which Meyer could not have known anything in 1921: the Dead Sea sect, which regarded itself as 'chosen' but did not use the title of 'Father'. The title however was acclimatized in the Jewish liturgy and not used only by the 'chosen devout ones'.

About the same time Alfred Bertholet wrote his still frequently quoted *History of Hebrew Civilisation* where he asserts—like Meyer—that the scribes, 'pluming themselves on their familiarity with these externals [Law code and Temple], to an extent never before known, looked upon themselves as the *élite* of humanity in comparison with all who were outside of their ranks'.[68] This characteristic goes back as far as the prophet Hosea, according to whom a 'special marital relation'[69] existed between God and Israel, but—says Bertholet—Hosea was mistaken or he exaggerated. Bertholet however says nothing about the fact that this 'marital relation' is also described as 'adultery' —about which Israel certainly could not be proud.

Finally we come to the author who must bear the greatest responsibility for the wrong view of Judaism in recent studies. This is Emil Schürer. He remains *the* authority on whom scholars and students prefer to rely; although G. F. Moore as long ago as 1921, in the article quoted at the opening of the present book, drew attention to the many basic mistakes and errors in his work. For Schürer 'the religious ideas of Israel in the age of Christ are on the one hand quite fantastic and on the other purely academic'.[70] The religious development of Judaism during this period does not follow the teaching of the prophets, but is characterized 'partly by the dominance of an intemperate and not truly religious imagination and partly by the academic reflections of scholars. Both factors dominated the development to such an extent that true religious life lost its internal strength.'[71]

Later he quotes Moses Mendelssohn's thesis that Judaism had no dogmas and observes: 'It is very interesting to see how rabbinism and rationalism here go hand in hand. What is common to both is that they fail to understand the nature and value of truly religious faith.'[72] Even in the decisions of the great rabbis, who adapted the Judaism of Jesus' time and later to new conditions, he finds nothing new: 'There is no trace here of ideas of reform, as Jewish self-love would like us to think.'[73]

This then is late Judaism as portrayed by German theologians. That they are not alone may be shown by a few additional quotations from French authors. The first is M.-J. Lagrange, founder of the Ecole Biblique in Jerusalem, who might also be called the father of modern Catholic biblical study. Here he produces an argument which, oddly enough, no one else had thought of: 'Undoubtedly, as today, they [the Jews] had the monopoly in certain forms of trade, not to speak of the management of finance.'[74] How can he make this assertion for which there is not the slightest evidence? We must assume that he has applied the anti-Semitic arguments of his own milieu to the conditions of nineteen centuries ago. The use of the very unscholarly 'undoubtedly' (*sans doute*) seems to be intended to stifle discussion from the outset. In his other main work the

36

author begins with a fervent invitation to the Jews finally 'to get away from the isolation of a nationalistic religion in order to enter into the precincts of the Catholic Church'.[75]

He then speaks of the works on the same theme which appeared before his own and has nothing but praise and admiration for the authors mentioned here, particularly for Schürer and Wellhausen (whose work will be discussed later). G. F. Moore he finds too pro-Jewish for his agreement. He charges Moore with quoting only those Jewish sources which prove his thesis. As if the Christian authors did not also select their sources to suit their preconceived opinions, without however displaying Moore's objectivity and knowledge.

Lagrange condemns rabbinic exegesis in its totality after the usual comparison with Christianity: 'We observe that Judaism as a whole is confined within a structure of legalism.'[76] He seems to know nothing about *haggadah* or Jewish mysticism. So at the end he asserts: 'At least it is easy to observe that the trend of Judaism—especially Pharisaic Judaism—was not towards a more interior—or, one might say, more mystical religion.'[77]

Joseph Bonsirven too published what has become a classical work on that period, adopting from the outset the attitude of a judge who at every turn compares decadent Judaism with a much superior Christianity. Here we need only mention that he takes Matthew 5.43, 'You shall love your neighbour and hate your enemy', as the authentic view of Jewish love of neighbour, a love to be directed only to a member of one's own people. Meanwhile it has been shown that there is no such rule in Judaism, not even in oral teaching, and that this statement must be linked with the Qumran sect where in fact such a regulation is found, But for him 'hatred for enemies remains the ordinary and normal attitude [of Judaism], an attitude intensified and sharpened in post-biblical literature'.[78] He ends with the generalization that the following conclusions must be drawn from his description: it is a question here 'of a self-centred and hostile particularism, distrust of mysticism and supernatural ideas and activities, a kind of anthropocentrism which exaggerates man's dignity and the inviolability of his inner being even in regard to divine grace, an inclination to ritualism, a predilection for the sensible and material aspect of religion, a tendency to reduce morality to a department of law.'[79]

Unfortunately these opinions do not belong merely to the past, not even in France. Pierre Benoit, Rector of the Ecole Biblique and Editor of the *Revue Biblique*, one of the best known French biblical scholars of our time, fully shares them. But we shall come back to his work later.

What these authors say can be summed up briefly. The centuries between the Babylonian exile and the emergence of Christianity was a time of decadence, of internal and external decline for Judaism. It had no longer any history properly speaking, its faith was externalized and rigid, God had become a distant God and the prophetic message was forgotten. Late Jewish existence as 'temple community' lasted at most to A.D. 70. Judaism misunderstood and failed in its real task and consequently destruction came as a just punishment. But we are now faced with the historical fact that the Jewish people still exists. Most theologians pay no further attention to this fact. The few who bother at all about this survival see the continued life of the Jewish people as a merely material existence. The Jews are condemned to go on as a dispersed people until one day they acknowledge Jesus as Christ and Saviour.

3
Law and Legalistic Piety

As in the last chapter, we find here too a consistent line of argument: the law and its observance are condemned. The authors never use the word 'Torah', but only its pejorative Greek translation: *nomos*, 'law'. 'Torah' however means much more than 'law': it means instruction, path, God's word and call to Israel as his part of the covenant; it is also Israel's grateful response to this covenant. In the following quotations the Torah is made to appear in Jewish understanding merely as a collection of legal prescriptions and summed up in terms of works and their reward. This preconceived judgement assumes that un-merited grace and 'justification by works' are irreconcilably opposed to one another. Christ brings to mankind justifying grace by faith; the Jew on the other hand relies wholly on the strict fulfilment of the law by his own power as the way to God; he justifies himself so to speak.

Among all the well-known Old and New Testament scholars, so far as I know, there is only one who finds problematic the antinomy—usually ascribed to Paul—between life-giving grace and life-destroying devotion to the letter. Norbert Lohfink[1] wonders how far this idea of justification by works, apparently managing without the precondition of God's grace, is contained at all in the Old Testament and particularly in Deuteronomy. Although he does not want to contradict the traditional theological understanding of Paul—grace versus law—he has to admit that the law already presupposes God's gift of grace to men and indeed is itself grace. Judaism as seen in the light of the Bible is not aware of any works which do not depend on God's help, mercy, and goodness, if they are to be accomplished at all. The law is observed out of love for God and this love is proved in the observance. We can rightly appeal to John's Gospel in this respect where it is clearly and concisely stated: 'He who has my commandments and keeps them, he it is who loves me' (14.21) and 'If you keep my commandments, you will abide in my love' (15.10). It is the same with Judaism: the basic motive for fulfilling God's commandments is love, the response to his love for the people he chose for his covenant.

Nor is there any contradiction between grace and law in the rabbinical tradition. The word *hesed*, translated by 'grace' or 'loving mercy', is one of the key words of the Hebrew Bible (e.g., Exod. 34.6–7; Deut. 7.9; Isa. 49.8). Israel often broke the commandments, but God's grace remained. The *Mekhilta* (a Midrash on the Book of Exodus) interprets Exodus 15.13: 'You have been gracious to us, for we had no good works to show.' Why then do all Christian interpreters regard Israel's fulfilment of the commandments as proud, self-justifying human work, when the important thing also in Christianity is to keep the commandments, to act? All we can do here is to point out once more that it is always basically a question of the same polemic as that which broke out in the first century, when the Christian arguments were intended to show the obsolescence of Judaism and the superiority of Christianity. Since it was impossible and unnecessary for the pagan converting to Christianity to do so by way of Judaism and the Torah, the precepts which no longer counted for Christians were rejected. From then onwards it was only a step—already taken by Paul—to regard the precepts in themselves as obsolete and as completely invalid. If we regard the separate existence of Judaism as finished with the coming of Jesus of Nazareth, this step is logical.

Today however we must read the Gospels and Paul in the light of a Judaism which continues to exist after two thousand years and take into account both its internal development and its history. But this is just what the authors mentioned here (not a complete list, but sufficiently representative of the still prevailing Christian attitude) fail to do. They teach as if they were still living in the first century, completely ignorant of the true nature of Judaism, which cannot be discovered solely from the New Testament writings, marked as these are already by the Jewish–Christian polemic. The old method of comparison, based on an essentially fundamentalist understanding of the biblical writings and a superficial, mostly second-hand knowledge of the Jewish sources, leads to the continuance of the basic misunderstanding of what the Torah means for the Jews: that it is not a question of self-satisfied legalism, but of obedience in love. The persistent lack of understanding becomes only too clear from the quotations given here.

Even such an outstanding expert on New Testament times as Joachim Jeremias could write as recently as 1971: 'Why does Jesus reject the *Halakah*? Mark 7.6–8 gives the answer. It is because this lawgiving is entirely the work of men (v.7) and contradicts the commandment of God (v.8). It puts casuistry above love, as Jesus shows by means of the *gorban* casuistry of the Rabbis (7.9–13).'[2] Jeremias, like most of his colleagues, appeals to Strack/Billerbeck,[3] to whose interpretation of Jewish sources we shall have to return. Even today it is still not clear how this *qorban* example, of the son who evades responsibility for his parents without cogent reasons, got into the Gospel. There is no rabbinical teaching on the subject and it is in complete contradiction to the fifth commandment. Jewish interpretation of the Bible is described by Jeremias and many others as casuistry; but how indispensable and necessary it was from the very beginning is strikingly proved by the fact that the New Testament also has to be interpreted. We need only recall the Sermon on the Mount, which is impossible to follow if it is taken literally and consequently also requires a 'casuistic' interpretation.

The above quotation comes from a section which Jeremias calls 'The piety that separates from God'.[4] It is this piety which is the 'cancer' of Judaism.[5] It means that sin is no longer seen as rebellion against God, but is rendered innocuous and compensated by merit. 'Where sin is not taken seriously, men think too well of themselves. They become self-assured, self-righteous and loveless.'[6] They then no longer take God himself seriously. 'This is the situation of those confronted with catastrophe: they are stubborn and indifferent, and the pious live in self-righteous blindness, which makes them deaf to the gospel.'[7] How does Jeremias reach his conclusion on Jewish piety? Since the Jews by and large were 'deaf to the gospel', they must have been stubborn and blind and self-righteous as a result of keeping their laws. So great a scholar ought to have allowed for the fact that the situation at that time was far more complicated and demands a more discriminating interpretation than that which emerges from the Gospels themselves.

Hans Werner Bartsch mentions only in passing: 'It is Israel's law which guarantees the existence of this people.'[8] But this simplifying judgement does not correspond to the facts: Israel always thought that God's love freely granted to his people and the people's covenant with him were and are the guarantee of its existence.

Georg Fohrer informs Israel that its understanding of the law is wrong: 'Even irreproachable fulfilling of the law means nothing. For man makes use of it constantly to claim rights as against God instead of acknowledging his will; by fulfilling the law he wants to secure God's recompense.... But what is really wanted is personal devotion more than objective achievement and external fulfilment. We must not stop at the letter of the law, but give life to the rigid commandment and fulfil it in spirit.'[9] This is wholly the authentic Jewish understanding of the law, but give life to the rigid commandment and fulfil knows very well that purely external observance is worthless—as worthless as the fulfilling of a precept for the sake of the reward. So we read in the commentary on Deuteronomy 11.13: 'I want to learn the Torah in order to be rich, or to be called Rabbi, or to gain a reward. But Scripture says: "You shall love the Lord, your God." Whatever you do, do nothing except out of love' (*Sifre–Deuteronomy* 41).

Fohrer is convinced that Israel failed God just because of its confidence in fulfilling the law: 'Israel, however, has failed to perform its divine task, because it wanted to make use of God merely as metaphysical security to live its independent life. The elements of this life, denied to God, are worship, law, nation and wisdom.'[10] Israel's 'whole life is ruled by this law' and 'by this law man's relationship to God is no longer characterized as submission in faith and trusting fellowship, but as a juridical bond. Man satisfies the divine requirements and thus secures his reward. And since it is not a question of complete obedience, perceiving and fulfilling the spirit of the precept, but only of external observance, there remains scope for independent decisions—as long as no regulation stands in the way.'[11] So there are not too many, but too few commandments? 'The most significant feature of Judaism remains its legalism':[12] as proof of this the author cites the Scripture reading in the synagogue and the veneration of the Torah-rolls. As further evidence of the strictly regulated 'legalistic piety', the author mentions scornfully how the Jew according to the Talmud has to dress; he continues: 'Only when it is a question of life and existence may the Jew infringe individual laws or set himself above most regulations. Here too we see the striving for security of life.'[13] To observe laws means 'securing one's life' in regard to God, infringement of particular laws in danger of death is cowardice. Can the Jew ever be right?

Fohrer then comes to speak of more recent times and shows the same biased misunderstanding: 'As protest, however, against this legalism, the Jewish revival movement of the Hasidim (the "devout") emerged in Eastern Europe as a parallel to the Pietism of the reformed Churches. It sought to understand the law from within and to teach people to keep it in spirit. In prayer and dancing people tried to lay themselves open for the reception of the divine Spirit as a gift of grace.' It is a question here of 'an artificially produced receptivity'.[14] One might think that the author was speaking of dancing dervishes, not of the Hasidim inwardly possessed by God.

Fohrer speaks equally contemptuously of Zionism. Again it is a question of 'making life secure' as in the time of the Old Testament. That ally is chosen who promises 'advantages and security. Again a national state has been established ... Again in certain circles there is a desire to make the law into a rule for the whole of life. Thus a situation is restored which resembles that in which Israel once failed. Will Judaism now do better?'[15] Note the familiar distinction between 'Israel' and 'Judaism'. Whether Judaism today as formerly will fail to do justice to its task is a purely rhetorical question for the author and must be answered with a decisive 'No', for 'neither is Zionism the solution to the Jewish question'.[16]

In his *History of Israelite Religion*, the author repeats himself.
Here he compares the prophetic message with the fulfilment
of the Torah, as if one excluded the other: 'The legal approach,
which we encounter towards the end of the pre-exilic period
and which is often associated with the cultic approach, may
likewise be said to have been surmounted by the prophetical
movement.'[17] Fohrer finds Israel's mistaken attitude to God
as existing already in the eighth century B.C. 'Seen from the
viewpoint of the prophets' message, fulfilment of the law
appeared merely as a further attempt on the part of the devout
individual to place Yahweh under an obligation through his own
actions.'[18] What does the author think of the many prophetical
utterances which, in opposition to his own thesis, constantly
exhort Israel to fulfil the law (cf. Amos 2.4; Isa. 58.13)? 'Personal
commitment must replace objective performance and merely
outward obedience.'[19] How can this be disputed for the
Deuteronomistic, especially the post-Exilic time whose main
principle, constantly repeated in one form or another, is: 'You
shall love the Lord your God with all your heart, with all your
soul, with all your might'? None of this counts for him: 'In
the schema of performance and reward man asserts his rights
vis-à-vis Yahweh instead of acknowledging Yahweh's will,
before which he is nothing. Therefore the prophetical message
excluded legalistic piety even in its more refined form, not to
mention its grosser manifestations.'[20] There seems to be little
point here—even if it were practically possible—in investigating
the prophetic pre- and post-Exilic message to see how profoundly it seeks to link internal attitudes with the observance
of the law in practical life. Fohrer himself confirms this at a
later stage, without however in any way changing his conclusion.

First of all, he says quite rightly that the truth of this legalistic
piety, as it is clear particularly from the psalms, lies in the
recognition of the unity of faith and life, of faith and action:
'A faith that does not lead to conclusions about what a man
must do and what a man must not do is dead.'[21] But what
follows is not so good: a Jew has no idea of the impossibility
of not sinning, of the *non posse non peccare*. He feels that he
is righteous and deserves his reward: 'The doctrine of retribution

in turn makes it easy to understand the insistence on one's own innocence, which the suppliant wanted to see confirmed so as not to appear rejected by Yahweh in the eyes of the multitude.'[22] Has the author never consulted a Jewish prayer book, never—for example—read the cantor's prayer on the Day of Atonement, before the Musaf liturgy: 'O behold me, destitute of good works ... standing in thy presence to supplicate thee for thy people Israel who have deputed me and, although I am not properly qualified for it, yet do I beseech thee O God of Abraham, Isaac and Israel, O Lord God merciful and gracious'?

Herbert Braun knows the Jewish ideas about God, whose attributes are both mercy and justice and who demands the fulfilment of the law. His interpretation, however, of how this was understood in Israel is strange: 'This bipolarity results in a peculiar uncertainty of attitude: the devout man is cheerfully confident that he can face the judgement with his achievements ... but at the same time he has the gnawing anxiety that these achievements may nevertheless not be adequate.'[23] 'It is the prospect of this judgement which leads to a continual oscillation between cheerfulness and anxiety. A rabbi can therefore recommend people to calculate the effects of transgression and obedience in terms of earthly advantage and eternal disadvantage, of earthly disadvantage and eternal advantage. The rabbi produces an example to show that God calculates just like a tradesman who keeps an exact record of his customer's debits and credits.'[24] Has not Braun here deliberately interpreted a metaphor all too literally? 'Faith in God', he continues, 'is here faith in a precisely worked out retribution and in the light of this conviction the pious Jew thinks he can behave in a way that will enable him to survive the judgement. Not, of course, without God's mercy. Mercy, however, does not turn everything radically upside down, but merely adjusts the balance —which man cannot quite attain—between achievement and reward.'[25] Nevertheless, 'despite the express assurance that God is no respecter of persons, the pious Jew expects special treatment for himself, as long as he has taken the law seriously. God is the personification of the law, which grants the pious

Jew a special religious status.'[26] What is the meaning, in this view, of the words of the prophet Amos: 'You only have I known of all the families of the earth; *therefore* I will punish you for all your iniquities' (Amos 3.2), if not that the 'special status' of the Jew carries with it not a privilege, but a greater involvement?

We constantly find an arbitrary selection of a few rabbinical texts which are then interpreted without regard for the interconnection in Judaism of covenant, mercy, and law, for the humble attitude of the truly devout man before God, of which hundreds of examples can be found in talmudic and liturgical texts. No importance is attached to these things: all that matters is to compare the God of mercy of the gospel with the God of strict retribution of Judaism.

Andrea van Dülmen published a monograph on *Die Theologie des Gesetzes bei Paulus*. From her standpoint the conclusions she reaches are intelligible. But it is just as wrong to try to ascertain the Jewish idea of the law from Paul as to judge Pharisaism by its portrayal in the Gospels. Thus she writes: 'The law of Christ dissolves the Mosaic law as an expression of the divine will and as norm in the life of the believer. The Mosaic law, as law for *Israel*, as a demand for works which cannot be satisfied by man, comes to an end with Christ: its intention, its totally binding character, its absolute claim are, however, taken up into the law of Christ.'[27] In Christ all that was hitherto valid in Judaism is abolished and fulfilled. 'As the law comes to an end in Christ only in so far as its attachment to the old aeon is broken and the law brought to its properly spiritual nature, so it is also with all the other means of salvation of the time before Christ: the election of Israel, descent from Abraham and circumcision, the covenant of God.'[28] All that constituted the real value and status of Judaism was taken over by Christ, transformed and dissolved with the new age which begins with him. 'As the advantages of the Jews for salvation remain also in the new age in the form of the new Israel, new covenant, spiritual descent from Abraham and circumcision of heart, so too the law of Christ holds in the new age in place of the Mosaic law.'[29] But nothing is said about the continuing

validity of the law for those—a whole nation—who did not
accept the 'law of Christ', but remained faithful to the covenant
concluded with God. As spiritual law 'it has entered into the
nomos tou Christou, while the [old] law in its fleshly character
is abolished. This distinction within the law is between the letter
that kills and the life-giving spirit.'[30] In Judaism it is a question
of the 'letter that kills' as opposed to the 'life-giving spirit'.
'The law in the old aeon is ... a law of works, a law of sin
and death', but in the new age 'the same law is spiritually ...
law of life, of grace and of faith.' Logically she concludes: 'A
distinction between the law according to the letter and the law
according to the spirit corresponds to the relationship between
the Mosaic law and the law of Christ.'[31]

The fundamental mistake of this author is that, like so many
others, she considers Paul's statements about the Jewish law
only from the Christian standpoint and leaves completely aside
the Jewish understanding of its Torah. At the same time no
regard is paid to the fact that the 'law' in Judaism is not by
any means a deadly observance of the letter, but behind every
law there is a spiritual confrontation with God, the lawgiver.
It is true that for someone who believes in Christ the law is
abolished and in fact replaced by the law of Christ. But
nothing is said about the position of those for whom the law
of Christ has not dissolved the law of Moses, except that the
latter is the 'letter that kills' or the 'law according to the flesh':
in other words, it has no longer any value.

Günther Schiwy too in his *Weg ins Neue Testament* says quite
clearly: 'Israel, the ancient people of God ... although it ...
pursued a law ... which God had given in order to prepare
the life of righteousness from Christ, did not in fact reach this
fulfilment of the law ... and thus did not come to Christ. Why
not? Because the Jews did not want to gain righteousness by
faith ... by surrender to Christ, but wanted to bring it about
themselves ... as it were by good works.'[32]

'The Mosaic law was meant to prepare precisely for this
righteousness through faith in Christ, so that in this sense Christ
is not only the end but also the goal of the Mosaic religion:
with Christianity the latter is abolished and transcended.'[33]

After this the situation of this Mosaic religion is clear: it rests on a culpable misunderstanding, an insistence on the 'old' law, and for two thousand years it has been on a wrong track through its own fault. The author makes his commentary too simple: he overlooks the complex problem of the person of Christ, whose recognition was not possible to the Jews and indeed was not required of them in the first century or later. Moreover he shows his ignorance of Judaism, which does not teach at all that anyone can attain to righteousness without God's aid and gracious love (*hesed*).

Werner Förster regards the law in the same way as the other theologians. From the time of Ezra onwards external actions like the observance of the Sabbath and circumcision acquired 'the status of confessional acts' and consequently 'the danger of degeneration into purely external piety was a growing menace. And this danger has gone along with Judaism ever since.' It attaches importance to action, to 'outwardly ascertainable things', but little importance to 'the weightier matters of the law, justice and mercy and faith'. Judaism has got its priorities wrong and has therefore succumbed to 'the sheer overwhelming might of external piety'.[34] This legalistic piety results in serious character-defects: 'The more the Law was viewed as the sum of specifiable obligations, the fulfilment of which required only a good will ... the more did election become for the pious a ground for pride and glory.'[35] Was anyone in Judaism ever regarded as 'pious' if he boasted of fulfilling the law and was proud of it? Is it not a wilful misunderstanding to assume that Rabbi Akiba maintains that everything depends on man's action when he gives the example: 'The shop stands open and the shopkeeper gives credit and the account-book lies open and the hand writes' (*Aboth* 3.17)? From the context it is clear that the example is meant to show that man is free and chooses his own fate, since we read in the preceding paragraph: 'All is foreseen, but freedom of choice is given; and the world is judged by grace, yet all is according to the excess of works (good or evil)' (3.16). Is it not a question here of seeking a balance between God's providence and mercy on the one hand and man's good will on the other, which can finally be proved only by his own

48

acts? The right understanding depends on the position adopted *a priori*. For Förster the whole legal system meant 'that the fulfilments of the commandments are written on the "credit side" and the transgressions on the debit side'.[36] Why should the fulfilment of God's commandments be regarded as a kind of horse-trading in Judaism, but in Christianity as a sign of loving devotion? Does not the parable of the last judgement (Matt. 25) show that in Christianity also a man is judged by his deeds?

Martin Metzger in his widely read book, *Grundriss der Geschichte Israels*, repeats Förster's judgement: 'Israel strove zealously for salvation; but, since it turned the law into a means of self-assertion and sought righteousness in virtue of its own achievement, it was scandalized by the Crucified, refused to listen to the message of justification by faith, and—blind to God's gift—passed salvation by.'[37] It has nothing to do with the law that Israel could not see in Jesus the Messiah: to charge Israel with lack of faith is to misunderstand its whole history from Abraham to our own time. How did this nation begin to exist and how does it continue to exist under the most intolerable conditions, if not by its faith, *emunah*, which implies steadfast trust in God and hope in his mercy?

Günther Schiwy in an earlier volume compares 'Blessed are the merciful, for they shall obtain mercy' (Matt. 5.7) with the Old Testament 'He who pursues righteousness and kindness will find life and righteousness and honour' (Prov. 21.21). 'This sounds too much like late Judaist legalistic piety, as if God had to reward even in this life anyone who had staked his claim by almsgiving.'[38] This is a striking example of an interpretation arbitrarily imposed on a text. 'Life, righteousness, and honour' can be related to the end-time, just as the Christian 'mercy'— as the author interprets it—is experienced by man only at the end of time. He speaks of 'late Judaist legalistic piety', for 'the law was not felt as a burden at the beginning or as long as people were aware that it could be fulfilled only with God's help and prayed for this. Thus the law was a gift of God's love, intended to awaken man's loving response.'[39] Unfortunately he does not stick to this correct understanding of the law as gift, but goes

on to say that in the later time 'a meticulous, timorous observation of the law was inculcated' and the devout person began
to lose 'sight of God himself behind the law'.[40]

The work of Leipoldt and Grundmann, *Umwelt des Urchristentums*, dates Judaism's changed attitude to the law from the
time of the Maccabees onwards. From this time Judaism's faith
and zeal are oriented 'no longer directly to Yahweh, but to his
law'. Even if the Jew is prepared to sacrifice his life, this is
not to be ascribed to his unselfish love of God, but is 'linked
with the confidence of thus being specially pleasing to God'.[41]
Jesus' zeal is confident and serene, while Jewish zeal is calculating and aimed at gaining a reward. Even the charitable works
recommended to the Jews point 'to the great importance which
divine recompense for human work possesses for the Pharisees.
Observances of the law produce a positive value for the agent,
transgressions a negative value. God is frequently seen in the
metaphor of a tradesman with his book-keeping and accounting:
a metaphor which occurs also in Jesus' parables—there,
however, in order to be transcended. Every fulfilment of the
law is entered on the credit side, every transgression on the
debit side.'[42] The principle is that the deed must be done to
obtain the reward. This is in direct contradiction to what ought
to have been known to the authors: as it is expressed in *Aboth* 1.3,
'Be not like slaves that minister to the Master for the sake of
receiving a bounty, but be like slaves that minister to the Master
not for the sake of receiving a bounty.'

Romano Guardini too adopted without any reservations this
view that a change took place in Judaism in the second century
B.C., from the idea of unselfish service to that of works produced in view of a reward: 'Thus the covenant founded on faith
and grace, that wonderful exchange of loyalty for loyalty, of
trust for divine aid, became a documented charter of rights and
demands.' Fundamentally it is a question of hypocrisy: 'On the
outside, greatest delicacy of conscience; on the inside, hardness
of heart. Outer loyalty to the Law; inner sin.'[43] Guardini's
intention, like that of his predecessors and successors, was to
explain Jesus' rejection by the Judaism of his time, and this
author—like the others—came to the conclusion that the Jewish

faith in these two centuries between the Testaments must have undergone a development for the worse. This is a postulate usually drawn from the Gospel texts. But these texts are not intended to give an exact picture of Judaism at that time, but mainly to arouse and strengthen faith in the person of Jesus. When Guardini, like many others, quotes the Gospels (e.g., Matt. 15.7; 22.19; 23.12–35), he overlooks the fact that these reflect a later and more acute controversy and do not present an objective picture of contemporary Judaism. Guardini takes the Gospels as a faithful mirror of events and concludes: 'What a terrible perversion of the divine has taken place—how terrible, is perhaps most apparent in the Pharisees' reply to the supreme authority of Roman law ... "We have a Law, and according to that Law he must die" (John 19.6–7). So infernally perverted has the law of God become, that his own Son must die by it.'[44] Such an uncritical view of the trial of Jesus in the interpretative Gospel of John can by no means be taken as a faithful picture of the Jewish view of God and the law. Incidentally, Guardini—in his eagerness to explain the condemnation of Jesus by Pilate—has got the Pharisees involved, although in this Gospel they do not play any part in the trial of Jesus. It should also be stressed that in this trial it was not a question of 'God's Son' either for the Jews or for the Romans: this title is used by the evangelists only for the risen Jesus.

Joachim Jeremias in *The Parables of Jesus* goes back to the Jewish model of the parable of the workers in the vineyard (Jerusalem Talmud, *Berakhoth* 2.3c) and compares it with Jesus' parable (Matt. 20.1–16). He reaches the conclusion that in the Gospel it is a question only of the goodness of the employer— God—but in the Jewish parable it is a question of the worker who has done enough in two hours to earn a full day's wages. Jeremias has misunderstood the point of the Jewish parable. The latter is a commentary on Ecclesiastes 5.12, 'Sweet is the sleep of a labourer', and seeks to show that it is not the duration of the work but the zeal with which it is accomplished which counts with God, and that even the person who dies young can receive the same reward as one who has a long life behind him. For we read there that God took him away from the work and 'walked with him'. But, since the comparison between rabbinic teaching and Gospel must *a priori* turn out to the disadvantage of the former, Jeremias concludes: '[Here] lies the difference between two worlds: the world of merit, and the world of grace; the law contrasted with the gospel.'[45] On the contrary, neither in the rabbinic nor in Jesus' parable has the worker earned his wages; in both cases he owes them to God's magnanimity.

According to Heinrich Schlier, the law has become a trap for the Jews and they are caught in it. He sums it up in this way: 'In their life encompassed by the law and yet disobedient to the law, they incur the wrath of God which is now hovering above them and will overwhelm them on the day of retribution.'[46] And again later: 'This zeal [for the law], however, is a jealous insistence on being able to face God. . . . In their deeds therefore they accept God's directions, but in their hearts they hold back. At the very point where they follow the Torah, they offend the Torah.'[47] Their obedience leads only to self-righteousness. Israel 'got entangled in the meshes of the law. For a long time it had turned God's Torah into a law demanding achievements, righteousness of faith into self-righteousness, works of love into material success.'[48] He goes a step further and asserts that the Jews at heart do not seek God 'but themselves', so that, 'contrary to their own knowledge and striving, they hate God'.[49] Does the author not see how he contradicts himself? If the Jews do not observe the law, they are disobedient; but if they observe it in their deeds, this is 'self-righteousness' and they prove by it that they 'hate' God. How then does he explain the words in John's Gospel (15.10): 'If you keep my commandments, you will abide in my love'? How paradoxical! If the Jew keeps God's commandment, this proves that he 'hates' God; if a Christian does so, this is a sign of his love for God.

Walter Grundmann explains that the Jew makes no distinction between the commandments and observes them without even wanting to know their meaning: 'Man's conduct under these conditions acquires the character of stern obedience, without understanding what is commanded.'[50] But how then can the scribe in particular ask Jesus about the great commandment and, on receiving the answer that it is love of God and neighbour (Deut. 6.4; Lev. 19.18), reply: 'You are right, Teacher, these are the great commandments and more important than all sacrifices' (Mark 12.28–34)? Piling up quotations continually in the same terms and with the same expressions becomes monotonous: 'God's commandment is used by them [the Jews] for self-exaltation and self-esteem. For them what matters is not God, but their own righteousness.[51] Through Jesus 'even the law of Moses and the piety based on it ... are revealed in their provisional character and thus brought to an end'.[52] For this law has led only 'to unbrotherliness, to contempt and hatred for the other person'.[53] All that the Jew wants to attain with the law is the 'reward' in one way or another, but 'Jesus liberates men from the oppressive burden of the law and acts not as the severe teacher, judging and censuring, but as God's envoy bringing freedom and aid'.[54] In Judaism oppressive burdens, in the gospel liberating grace. None of these theologians can get rid of this wrong conception of Judaism's understanding of the law: the contrast is based on a preconceived judgement which merely needs to be proved. Behind this biased judgement lie ignorance of Judaism as it really is and arbitrary interpretation of the texts.

For Martin Noth the 'true Israel' ceased to exist as early as the Babylonian captivity. All that remained was for the law to be turned into an independent reality, taking the place as it were of God himself. Only at this stage did the concepts of merit and penalty, the whole idea of retribution and legalistic piety for the sake of merit, emerge in Judaism. 'The gradual making absolute of "the law" must be looked on as a false track, which led to consequences which led right away from the authentic foundation of faith.'[55] It is not much of a consolation to be told that in all institutions in the course of time statutes may be made absolute and that all men—as in the paradigmatic example of the Jews—'worship dead ordinances and statutes'[56] long after they have lost their original value.

Eduard Lohse writes very much in the same way: 'This law, which ruled the life of the Jew in an abundance of individual precepts and prohibitions, was no longer understood as God's living word but had become a rigid, firmly outlined factor.'[57] Hence 'the argument which Jesus had to settle with the Jews ... broke out about the understanding of the Jewish law, which allows no scope for God's freely granted mercy'.[58] This is scarcely confirmed by the Gospels. Certainly the most acute argument between the primitive Church and the Synagogue was about the duration and value of the law for *Christians*; but Jesus himself and his disciples lived under the law. For this author the law involves 'the greatest threat which can seize on man: the desire to boast before God of success attained by one's own strength, in virtue of the law, in fulfilling and mastering one's life'.[59] When did a pious Jew—not the Pharisee caricatured in the parable of the publican—ever boast of fulfilling the law by his own power? The prayers in the psalms show him always as coming before God as a beggar in need of grace, just because he confesses that he is a sinner and cannot satisfy God's commandments if he is left to himself.

Does Martin Dibelius really know what he calls 'Jewish theology'? It 'claims to explain all the fortunes of life, happiness as well as suffering, by reference to divine retribution'.[60] But 'God's dealing with men cannot be confined within the mathematics of a pure doctrine of recompense.'[61] Would any of the Jewish authorities who accepted the Book of Job into the Canon of the Bible ever have asserted this principle or ever lived in accordance with it? Are there not rabbinical commentaries with a very different sound? For instance, *Sifre–Deuteronomy* 26: 'Israel had two good leaders, Moses and David. All their sins could have been compensated by good works; but they prayed to God out of his mercy to be gracious to them and forgive them. How much more should one of their most unworthy students therefore pray to God to forgive him gratis, out of mercy.' Or the fine interpretation of Exodus 33.19: 'God showed him [Moses] all the treasures in which the rewards of the righteous are stored away.... Later he saw a huge treasure and inquired: "Whose is this great treasure?" The Divine rejoinder was: "... Unto him that hath not, I have to supply freely and I help him from this great pile, as it says, AND I WILL BE GRACIOUS TO WHOM I WILL BE GRACIOUS,

namely to whom I wish to be gracious. Similarly, AND I WILL
SHOW MERCY ON WHOM I WILL SHOW MERCY"' (*Midrash
Rabbah*, Exodus Ki Thissa, xlv, 6).

Nevertheless, Dibelius is convinced of his thesis: 'Jesus and
his disciples lived in daily contact with a system of piety that
was built on a rational computation of the relation of man to
God, and thereby set itself up over God.'[62] For him the whole
Bible seems to be identical with 'law': 'The strict Jewish piety
of Jesus' day rested upon the interpretation of the Bible ...
He did not derive his own message from the Bible. The Law
with its precepts could have become for men the occasion for
recognizing the absolute will of God. But men have defrauded
themselves of this opportunity by their expansion of the precepts
into a legal system.'[63] Today it is generally recognized that Jesus
himself and the evangelists who interpreted him derived at least
part of his message from the Bible and from the rabbinical
understanding of Scripture. None of this is derogatory to the
person and proclamation of Jesus. While acknowledging all that
is new in the Gospel, it is impossible not to find a continuity
with what we know as the Old Testament. This is the line
increasingly adopted by modern New Testament scholars.
Dibelius' works go back to the twenties and betray the influence
of Harnack, who wanted to separate the New Testament from
the Old.

After his emigration, Paul Tillich lived and taught in the
United States; but he too could not get away completely from
the theory of Jewish legalism which had become acclimatized
mainly in German theology. In his *Systematic Theology* he
writes: 'Most conspicuous and important for the history of
religion are the legalistic ways of self-salvation. Judaism is right
in contending that obedience to the law is not legalism. The
law is, first of all, a divine gift; it shows to man his essential
nature, his true relationship to God, other men, and himself
... But it does so in terms of commandments, just because man
is estranged from what he ought to be. This is the possibility
and temptation of legalism. It is an almost irresistible temptation. Man, seeing what he ought to be, driven by the anxiety
of losing himself, believing in his strength to actualise his

essential being ... tries again to attain what he has lost ... Whenever attempted, legalism as a way of self-salvation has come to catastrophe.'[64] This was the case in Judaism at the time of Jesus and its tragic *hubris* brought on the catastrophe.

In his *Jesus of Nazareth* Günther Bornkamm speaks of 'that formalistic legalising of the law, and a corresponding detailed technique of piety, to which Jesus' message of the divine will stands in sharp contrast. The nature and spirit of the later Judaism of the Talmud have their origin here.'[65] Thus the Judaism of the Christian era is analysed and condemned in one sentence. He returns again to this 'understanding of the law': through the works required by the law 'the great reckoning with God begins: reckoning and counter-reckoning; merit and debt; reward and punishment; the actions of men being bartered in transaction with God. ... What does this conception of the law reveal? Evidently this: the law has become separated from God and has become man's real authority. It no longer leads to a meeting with God, but rather frustrates it. ... God is concealed behind the law and man behind his achievements and works.'[66]

This interpretation makes a completely undiscriminating and false accusation against Jewish religious mentality, which in fact looks to the law only as the way to encounter with God himself, for whom all achievements are of no account. We read, for instance, in the closing prayer of the liturgy of the Day of Atonement: 'What are we? What is our life? What is our piety? What our strength? What our might? What shall we say before thee, O Lord our God and God of our fathers? ... And if a man be righteous, what can he give thee?' Here, as in the whole Jewish liturgy, we do not find a single instance of emphasis on deeds, on one's own works, but only the constantly repeated acknowledgement of one's own sins and confident trust in God's mercy and pardon. *Lex orandi—lex credendi*, the law of praying is the law of believing; the principle is particularly relevant here and it means that we do justice to Judaism only by quoting from these many prayers instead of fabricating a Christian system of a calculating Judaism, haggling with God—which does not square with the truth.

Rudolf Bultmann, the teacher of Bornkamm, is even more

explicit in his sharp condemnation of Jewish legalistic piety: 'The law as it confronts man in the form of the law of Moses is the way in which man comes to grief in sin. Christ is the end of the law.'[67]

He speaks in the same way in his *Theology of the New Testament*, which appeared a little earlier: 'As interpretation of the will, the demand, of God, Jesus' message is a great *protest against Jewish legalism*—i.e. against a form of piety which regards the will of God as expressed in the written Law and in the Tradition which interprets it, a piety which endeavours to win God's favour by the toil of minutely fulfilling the Law's stipulations.' In this way the 'motivation to ethical conduct is vitiated'.[68] Jewish obedience is purely formal, fulfilling the letter of the law, but not its real, moral demands. Whatever happens is the result merely of human vanity and thus obedience to the law is corrupt at its very roots. Seen as a whole, 'Judaism was no longer a cultic religion, but had become a religion of observance.'[69]

Leonhard Goppelt's work, *Christentum und Judentum* (abridged English edition, *Jesus, Paul and Judaism*), sees the main principle of Judaism in 'its confession to the God of the Old Testament and ... its life under the law', and this has been shaken 'to its very foundation' through and in the person of Jesus.[70] 'Jesus emphasized the permanence of natural law above the restricted validity of ceremonial law; ... He called for a genuine ethical concern in place of casuistry; ... He summarized all of the commandments in the commandment of love; ... He demanded "genuine, radical obedience in place of both ritualistic piety and a legal understanding of man's relationship with God" (cf. Bultmann).'[71] Here again we encounter the lack of understanding of Jewish ethics, which also gives priority over all the other commandments to love of God and neighbour (cf. Mark 12.28–34). 'Israel's striving for righteousness by the Law was, as Rom. 7 shows, inevitably *a striving for "their own righteousness"*. They were really seeking what the brother of the prodigal son was seeking, not unification with the Law but rather their own worthiness.'[72] Israel's 'ignorance is not a tragic mistake, but rather a guilty blindness that also characterizes the

religious efforts of the Gentiles (Eph. 4.18 . . . Rom. 10.14–18)'.[73]
If Paul's theology is accepted without more ado as a historically
exact description of the Jewish understanding of the law, not
compared with Jewish sources, regardless of the fact that Paul
was concerned with Christian theology and not with an objective
portrayal of the Jewish way of faith, we can scarcely be surprised
at the author's conclusions. At any rate we must charge him
in his book, which is supposed to be about Christianity and
Judaism, with completely failing to pay attention to Jewish self-
understanding and with judging Judaism solely in the light of
a purely Christian theological standpoint.

In his article 'Nomos' in the *Theological Dictionary of the
New Testament* Walter Gutbrod shows a certain understanding
of the way in which the importance of the law is subordinated
to the covenant: 'Observing the Law does not create the
relation to God; it keeps the people in this continuing relation,
e.g. 2 Ch. 33.8.' But he adds at once: 'In fact, however, the
emphasis and concern rest increasingly on the second aspect,
so that everything depends on observance of the Law.'[74] At
first the Torah was the revelation of the special relationship
of Israel to its God: 'For all practical purposes the Torah comes
fully to the forefront, primarily as the Law which claims the
will of man.'[75] He further explains that the Torah was indeed
revelation but that it was confronted by the perfect revelation
in Jesus: 'In the Law, in Scripture, Jesus is attested and promised
as the Christ ... What the Law says or ordains is fulfilled in
the life and work of Jesus.'[76] At this point there ought to have
been an explanation that the evangelists apply the Old Testament
a posteriori to Jesus.

Erik Peterson, at one time professor of Protestant theology,
later a convert to Catholicism, lectured in the thirties at the
summer schools of the University of Salzburg. Three of these
lectures were published in book form as *Die Kirche aus Juden
und Heiden*, which is still often quoted. There he says: 'If the
Church and not the Synagogue is the true Israel, then the
Church's interpretation of the Scriptures is the true one as
opposed to the exegesis of the Synagogue. This undoubtedly
is most decisively expressed in the interpretation of the "law",

for in the last resort the Jew will be able to understand only carnally even the fulfilment of all precepts of the law.'[77] The whole lecture places Israel in the sharpest contrast with the Church: a contrast and a conflict which will end only with the conversion of the Jews.

The works produced in the twenties are those most used as sources by later writers. One of these is the work of W. Bousset and H. Gressmann, *Die Religion des Judentums im späthellenist-ischen Zeitalter*. The attitude of these two to the law is un-equivocally and harshly expressed; Judaism becomes 'a religion of observance and absolute persistence. Christianity becomes the heir of Judaism.'[78] 'The piety of these leading classes was bound gradually to become very superficial. Cult, in the hands of this priesthood, was essentially something ingeniously worked out and artificially constructed ... it was marked by a barren formalism.'[79] What we have here is 'a routine piety, a purely formal observance',[80] ending in moral ruin. This idea of moral ruin is found particularly in these early authors; it is never clear where they get it from, unless they base it on certain Gospel sayings which cannot be confirmed from other sources: for instance, those referring to the exploitation of widows; the son's refusal, under pretext of *qorban*, to support his parents. As a result of the thesis that late Judaism can scarcely be linked with the early Israelitic faith, it is now suggested that there is here a 'new religion'. This 'new religion was a religion of observance which had drawn into itself among many other things what remained of this inwardly rigid and almost dying cultic piety'.[81] Furthermore, the 'union of religion and law in the legal system became the decisive feature of the Jewish religion'.[82] Whatever does not suit this thesis is dismissed as exceptional. 'Hillel's fine words about "loving mankind and bringing them nigh to the Law" (*Aboth* 1.12) are merely propaganda.'[83] This is always the explanation of recommendations in rabbinical sources of humility, friendliness, gentleness, even to outsiders.

This motive poisons even what is best in Judaism; for 'the individualism of Jewish piety culminates in the hope of recom-pense in the next world'.[84] The work often adopts the method of Strack/Billerbeck and gives excellent quotations which prove the very opposite of the conclusions drawn from them. But this does not disturb the authors. For, 'with all these [ancient Jewish prayers expressing humility], we cannot, of course, forget how heavily burdened this piety was with externals, with the most trivial regulations and hairsplitting, with anxieties and doubts about ceremonial, which a tireless ingenuity had made into mountains'.[85] The effort to pile up different expressions for the same thing is amazing and would have been worthy of a better cause. In the five hundred pages of this work, which continues to be widely read and quoted, the authors repeat themselves *ad nauseam*. We read, for instance, that it has already been shown 'how the nature of Judaism as a religion of observance finds expression in the incapacity to distinguish the important from the unimportant, in the whole casuistic attitude, and finally in the negative basic orientation'.[86] But there is no hesitation in repeating it all once more: 'All this is linked with a certain lack of subjective truthfulness and sincerity, a striving after externals and appearances.'[87] God is 'judge and rewarder' and feared for that reason.[88] No importance is to be attached to the sublime idea of the *kiddush hashem* (sanctification of the divine name), say the two fundamental experts on Judaism.

G. F. Moore, even when he had only the second edition of the work (1906) at his disposal, accused Bousset of incompetence in his use of second-hand Jewish sources which he could not consult in the original. Bousset also relies on material drawn from the apocalyptic writings, which are not authoritative either for the Judaism of the first century or for the later normative Judaism. As Moore very rightly observes, this is rather like judging Christianity in the light of the apocryphal gospels. The authors have failed in their main concern which was to portray the 'religion of Judaism': it serves merely as background and contrast to the Christian faith so that the latter is made to appear so much more sublime.

The basic ideas of Adolf von Harnack are too well known for us to examine them in detail here. As Luther, following Marcion, rediscovered, the law is 'a "material law" which Christians no longer need. . . . The whole sphere of law as earthly is subject to the Christian and not the Christian to the law;

but as religious it belongs to a stage that is superseded. Anyone who does not recognize this must remain a Jew. But, since the law runs through the whole Old Testament, including the prophets, the book as a uniform whole is beneath Christendom.'[89] Harnack at least clears the table, sweeping aside the Old Testament; in a sense this is more honest than the inconsistent and often forced arguments which attempt to separate the religion of the prophets from that of the 'law' and change the former, believing Israel into a 'late Judaism' of a purely external observance.

Adolf Schlatter's tone and mode of expression are such that he must be accused not only of anti-Judaism, but of an unscholarly anti-Semitism. The distinction, however, is minimal with a number of scholars. 'Jesus rejected the self-confident claim of the Jew to his own greatness and showed him the hypocritical contradiction in which he became involved when he attempted to cover up his inward alienation from God by parading his veneration of the law and his fidelity to Scripture.'[90] Legalistic piety was 'mere appearance and the desires for which they struggled were exclusively selfish: they were fighting for money and women.'[91] This corresponds more to the anti-Semitism typical of the twenties of this century than to the Judaism of the first century.

Eduard Meyer too, a contemporary of Schlatter, stands out by the violence of his language. For Jesus it is, of course, obvious that the law must be observed, 'but as such, if the observance does not spring from an internal disposition, it is not only worthless appearance, but really spiritually ruinous'.[92] As a result of a more or less 'mechanical adjustment' to it, the law serves only to 'alienate man inwardly from God'.[93] Jesus turns the law into 'a religious ethic', something that the Jews had not been able to do, 'since they had neither the strength nor the courage to discard ritualism'.[94] The study of the law 'leads to sanctimoniousness and hardening of the heart; behind formal correctness worldly ambition and cupidity are concealed. . . . The traditions . . . often enough are in outright opposition to the law and force on it an interpretation which actually nullifies it (Mark 7.8f.).'[95]

In Alfred Bertholet's outdated *History of Hebrew Civilisation* we read, among other things: 'Law code and Temple lent each other mutual support, and this brought about a fateful increase in the value attached to the externals of religion. The fulfilling of the law viewed from the standpoint of retribution or requital gave rise to a type of piety characterized by a readiness to enter into reckoning with God.'[96] Piety thus becomes observance. This goes back to Ezra. From his time onwards 'ruthless objectivity' choked all warm-hearted humanity, for 'in the spirit of this new religious ideal of Ezra men sought to work out their salvation in fear and tremblings'.[97] Worship and sacrifice were detached from their natural roots in the nation: 'Instead of the festal joy which had hitherto found expression in eating and drinking before Yahweh we have now the terrible earnestness of a difficult obedience.'[98] Even the spiritualization of religion in worship and prayer is against 'nature'; it is no longer 'national'.

Each author seems to write from his own cultural-political standpoint. There is no attempt at an objective portrayal, to enter into the true spirit of Judaism, to understand its interiorization after the Exile, as it is expressed, for instance, in the psalms. We are completely justified in speaking of an *a priori* anti-Judaist attitude which sees in Judaism a discarded, even corrupt religious phenomenon, as opposed to a sublimely spiritual Christianity which makes the former appear to be completely overshadowed and worthless.

The two most important forerunners of modern German theology on Judaism should now be mentioned. For, although in other fields their studies are regarded as out of date, their successors have simply taken over what they said about Judaism and particularly the law without any noticeable modification. Julius Wellhausen in his book, *Israelitische und jüdische Geschichte*—the title alone is typical—writes as follows: in the second century B.C., Jewish piety 'became hardened and rigid'. It attached the greatest importance to 'forms and externals' and made no distinction 'between minor and major matters in the law'.[99] 'The works of morality were largely set aside; the works of sanctification, fasting, prayer, almsgiving preferred. But nothing was of value unless it was firmly regulated; the important thing was formal exactitude.'[100] The law did not only ruin morals, since 'service to neighbour had to come after the practices of godliness; it also despiritualized religion. Access to God was closed by convention. . . . A veritable idolatory of the law prevailed.'[101] Thus he reaches his final judgement: 'For the Jews there is no internal link between the good person and the good thing; the action of the hands and the aspirations of the heart fall apart. Pious activity has absolutely no earthly aim, but hope is so much more worldly; the unspeakable pedantry of godly practices and the ill-concealed cupidity of the devout person go together.'[102] It is a religion which reached its end with Jesus.

Emil Schürer is not troubled by doubts at all and is quoted as uncritically today as he always was. Fulfilling the law might have led to solicitous love, but it worked out differently: 'The whole piety of the Israelite consisted in observing in all its details the law given by God, with fear and trembling, with the zeal of a scrupulous conscience.'[103] For Judaism the whole Bible contains nothing but law: all its writings, 'for the Jewish consciousness, are primarily not admonitory and consoling, not edifying or historical books, but likewise "law", the embodiment of God's demands on his people.'[104] And 'anyone who does not know the law is accursed (John 7.49): this was the basic conviction of post-Exilic Judaism'.[105] Law was also the reason for the origin of the synagogue: 'The main purpose of these Sabbath assemblies in the synagogue was not divine service— that is, not worship—but religious instruction, and this for the Israelite is primarily instruction in the law.'[106] We may wonder whether Schürer ever saw a Jewish prayer book. He composed a special chapter on 'Life under the Law'.[107] All zeal in family, school, synagogue, was directed to making 'the whole people a people of the law'.[108] The motives and means involved were 'faith in divine retribution: a retribution in the most strict, juridical sense'.[109] The covenant also was thus 'understood in a purely juridical sense'. It is 'a legal contract . . . The nation is bound . . . to observe the law punctiliously and conscientiously; but God too is bound to award the promised recompense to the people according to the measure of their achievement'.[110]

The Jews are a nation of tradesmen even in religion.

'Good works ... therefore are like capital: we enjoy the interest in this life while the capital itself remains for the future life.'[111] Zeal for the law was wholly for the sake of recompense. The saying of Antigones of Soko (*Aboth* 1.3), that we ought not to be like servants who minister for the sake of a reward, is by no means true or typical of Judaism; for the Jews are exactly like slaves who minister for a reward.

There was no 'true piety, only external formalism'; prayer too was 'chained within a rigid mechanism'[112] and consequently became an external work. And finally 'prayer was reduced to being at the service of vanity' and was misused 'as a cover for inward corruption'.[113] The purity laws simply provided an occasion for 'treating the field of sexual life in a manner which closely resembles the slippery casuistry of the Jesuits'.[114] 'It was a terrible burden which a false legalism had loaded on to the shoulders of the people.' His proofs of this are Matthew 23.4 and Luke 11.46: 'At every step, in the exercise of one's calling, at prayer, at meal times, at home and on journeys, from early morning until late evening, from youth until old age, the coercive and deadly formula was dominant. Under such a burden it was impossible for a healthy moral life to flourish.... For anyone who took it seriously life was a continual torment ... And for anyone who had brought the understanding and manipulation of the law to a fine art, pride and vanity [were] almost unavoidable.'[115]

Scarcely any of the authors mentioned refers to Jewish sources or seems to be acquainted with them except in quotations from the very early Christian writers—for example, the Fathers of the Church—or in such an anti-Semitic work as *Das entdeckte Judentum* (1699) by J. A. Eisenmenger. The descriptions in the Gospels, attributable to the conflict of the early Church with Judaism, are regarded as objective descriptions of the Jewish view of life and religion. The authors are apparently unaware of a post-biblical, continually existing and developing Judaism or they give a deliberately distorted picture. Law and covenant are separated from each other: since the latter has ceased to exist, the former—no longer valid for Christians—

must be interpreted as evil and corrupt. There is no hint of the actual position of the law as man's grateful response to the covenant, as sanctification of the whole of daily life. Ignorance or prejudice, partly attributable to a fundamentalist exegesis of the Pauline epistles, blind Christians—not Jews—to the true nature of the law. We may, however, sadly wonder why Psalm 119, for example, does not convey to them anything of the joy, the jubilation and gratitude which the Jew from time immemorial has felt for the law.

This tendency is not restricted to Germany. It is evident also in the works of some of the best-known French specialists in the field of Judaism. One or two of these may be quoted here, for purposes of comparison. Marie-Joseph Lagrange, for instance, reproaches the Jews for being too little concerned with messianic ideas. The reason is that 'they appear to be so absorbed in their law and its traditions that the rest of the world does not seem to exist for them'.[116] In a later work in which he attempts to describe Jewish religion as a whole, he speaks of their relations with God also in prayer: 'The most baffling thing is that we find such admirable maxims in their writings and then observe that all their attention is directed to a set of regulations which they are determined to derive from the law.'[117] Whatever they have written, no matter how deep the ideas contained there, does not count. They have succumbed to legalistic piety. He does not tell us, however, how this contradiction can be explained, between the 'admirable maxims' and the purely external observance arising from a law which is not rightly understood.

Joseph Bonsirven describes in his first work how the Jews themselves have turned the law into a ghetto: 'A narrow spirit, obstinately shrivelled up within itself and peevishly hostile to all strangers; an intemperate, entangled legalism, set on continually forging new fetters on the one hand, and on the other dissipating all its strength in the vain agitations of its endless discussions, its inextricable casuistry.'[118] He says much the same thing a few years later. For, although he mentions that one of the motives of legalistic piety is obedience to God's will, he insists that the real reason for obedience is 'the fear of penalties and the hope of rewards'.[119] Judaism could only stagnate, for the dominant rabbinism 'stuck more blindly to the letter than to the spirit of the law, losing sight of the prophetical vision'. Out of the exaggerated cult of the Torah was born legalism and 'an inclination to ritualism, a predilection for the sensible and material in religion, the tendency to make morality a part of jurisprudence'.[120] Thus the multiplication of external observances—phylacteries, for instance—shows the 'final exaggeration of this attitude, the confusion of the frontiers between religion and superstition.'[121] The supernatural, mystical element of religion is crowded out by observances.

Much later, in the sixties, Pierre Benoit, rector of the Ecole Biblique in Jerusalem, admits that we can and must recognize the concept of grace in the Old Testament. The mistake lies in the fact that we 'are apt to judge the old dispensation in the light of the later Judaism which had vitiated everything with its belief that it was possible to keep the law by human effort alone'.[122] It was the fault of the Jews that, 'in its historical realisation, the system of the Law failed'. For, 'instead of remaining faithful to the true tradition of the saints of the Old Covenant, [they] ignored the need of divine help and looked for justification only from their own fulfilment of the Law, that is to say, in the final analysis, only from their own human efforts'.[123] The law has become one-sided observance, no longer part of the covenant, and consequently it can logically lead only to perdition. For—and this is continually stressed—the Jew relies on his own efforts in carrying out the commandments; God's help and grace are no longer given to him. He does not know this, however, and he flatters himself, contented and proud, that he has done all in his power to satisfy God's demands on the nation.

This should be sufficient evidence of the persistently disparaging interpretation, the one-sidedness, prejudice, and ignorance of these writers. It is clear from their very words. No further commentary is required.

4

Pharisees and Scribes

It is not easy to separate this chapter completely from the previous one, on the law, or to avoid repetition. For the members of both these groups—often incorrectly regarded as identical—are supposed by most commentators simply to represent the 'law'. It is even assumed that the law is in a sense their creation, as 'oral tradition' or 'tradition of the Fathers', emerging in the period between the Testaments and orally transmitted until it was finally recorded in the Talmud. Since however they are mostly represented in the gospel as *the* enemies of Jesus' teaching, in episodes and sayings which often give them a distorted or disfigured appearance, it seems appropriate to devote a special chapter to them.

This is all the more important since the picture of the Pharisees and scribes given in other historical sources does not correspond to that of the Gospels. It is impossible to explain in detail here the reasons for this contrast. We can only point out briefly that Jewry, after the destruction of the temple in A.D. 70, recognized the Pharisees and their rabbis as its natural religious leaders and the organization of the Jewish religion after the disasters of 70 and 135 as their work. The more the early Church came up against the opposition of the Jewish communities, the more urgent it became to portray them as the enemies of Jesus himself, since they were undoubtedly the opponents of the Christian mission and it was largely their opposition which led to the failure of that mission as a whole in the synagogue.

As as example we may cite Matthew 23, where Jesus accuses the Pharisees and scribes of every possible transgression and crime. A closer exegesis of this chapter however shows that it originated not so much in the preaching of Jesus as in the historical situation of Church and Synagogue and their controversies after the year A.D. 70. But the fact is that even those theologians who seek to understand the Gospels also in the light of the historical situation at the time of their final redaction and who fully admit the complexity of the sources which have been worked into the Gospels still continue to judge the 'Pharisees' and the 'scribes' as if the New Testament provided an objective description of their mentality and views. The excerpts here given, in the same chronological order as before, provide evidence of this.

Thus Jeremias in his latest work (1971) discusses the famous parable of the Pharisee and the publican as if it had been an actual event. The publican finds God's good pleasure (Luke 18.9–14), but not the Pharisee. Why? 'Because the pious are separated from God by their theology and their piety. For a piety that leads men astray to pride and self-assurance is an almost hopeless thing.'[1] In the 'woes', directed 'against the *Pharisees*', Jesus accuses them of being conscientious in small things, 'but setting at nought the great demands of God, righteousness, mercy and faithfulness (Matt. 23.23f.)'.[2] Externally they are clean, 'whereas within they are unclean, though the one and only thing that matters before God is inward cleanliness'. 'All their piety is at the service of their need to assert themselves and their ambition, and is therefore hypocrisy. So they are like graves which are whitewashed in the spring ... outside they are bright, but inwardly they are dead bones (Matt. 23.27f.).'[3] 'Where is it that Jesus sees the cancer that is not recognized by the pious men of his day? This becomes clearest in his sayings against the Pharisees, with whom he had most to do.'[4] Jeremias then insists that in the eyes of Jesus they are upright men, and we have no right to attribute to him a distorted picture of the Pharisees. And yet they are 'at a special remove from God', for '*they do not take sin seriously*'.[5] Pharisaic Judaism is aware of sin, but this is 'made innocuous by two things: by casuistry and the idea of merit.... The result of this casuistry is that sin is not seen as rebellion against God. The *idea of merit* makes sin innocuous in that a counter-balance is set over against it. Merits compensate for sins.... The only important thing is that in the final judgement merits should outweigh the transgressions. The Pharisee was convinced that this would be so in his case, but not in that of the sinners. This devaluation of sin by casuistry and the idea of merit has a disastrous consequence.'[6] Men think too well of themselves and 'become self-assured, self-righteous and loveless. The Pharisee was convinced that he belonged to the true people of salvation. He did not doubt for a moment that God's good pleasure rested on him and he was conscious of being superior to the sinner (Luke 18.11f.). This self-assurance, in Jesus' view, destroyed the whole of a man's life. The man who thinks too well of himself no longer takes God seriously.'[7] For the Pharisee all that matters is 'what men think of him. His whole piety ... thus becomes hypocrisy (Matt. 6.1–18).'[8] With Jesus this 'devaluation' of sin and contempt for the less devout brother comes to an end. As proof of the idea of compensating merit Jeremias quotes Strack/Billerbeck, i, pp. 429–31, 822d; the texts are partly drawn from apocalyptic writings and show nothing more than love and a deep fear of God.

Jeremias has got himself entangled in contradictions which he does not elucidate. He speaks of the Pharisee's serious obedience in trying to fulfil God's will and says expressly that we have no right 'to impute to him [Jesus] a distorted picture of the Pharisees',[9] and yet his description of their piety and mode of life is a distortion of the reality as known from other sources. The polemical problems involved in the gospel statements are also torn from their historical context and—we might say—understood in a fundamentalist sense. His documentation comes from the very one-sided work by Strack/Billerbeck; no other source outside the gospel is brought forward as a proof.

In his book, *Jesus*, Herbert Braun says that what the Pharisees are aiming at 'is the involvement of life as a whole in the co-ordinate system of the commandments'.[10] Consequently, in contrast to Jesus, they give doctrine priority over action. Jesus criticizes 'the contradiction between theory and practice with the scribes and Pharisees, not simply because it amounts to hypocrisy, but because the teachers of the law by their inconsistent behaviour fail to show love towards the people they teach'.[11] As proof of this Braun quotes Matthew 23.4,13.

Georg Fohrer has already been quoted sufficiently on the inadequacy of legalistic piety. He also explains that 'the form of pharisaic legalistic piety which prevailed as authoritative' is responsible for Judaism's wrong understanding of existence, which is typically human and not in accordance with the message of the prophets. 'Israel and Judaism, despite Moses, the prophets, and Jesus, failed in their task. But in this juxtaposition of task and failure the fate of Judaism is involved',[12] a fate which inevitably leads to disaster.

As already mentioned, Werner Förster has been trying sincerely for decades to get into the mind of Judaism. But he too has not succeeded in grasping the true spirit of Pharisaism. Thus he asserts that they shrink from all innovations and transmit only the traditions they have received: 'Any attempt to establish what is "right", i.e. what is God's will, in every individual case, leads to deductions which immediately contradict the essence of morality.'[13] The Pharisees wanted to give an example in their own behaviour of how people should live: 'This gave rise to the ostentatious piety that Jesus castigates in the Sermon on the Mount.'[14] Now Förster knows that there is a great deal in pharisaic literature which contradicts this statement, but he continues to defend it: 'It is a mistake to rely upon individual rabbinic writings without paying regard to their value in the appropriate context and in the sum-total of pharisaic ideas.'[15] But is not this the very method adopted by him and his colleagues, completely ignoring the wider scope of rabbinic literature and relying on individual examples torn from their context? He admits that 'Pharisaism was striving at that time to avoid becoming swamped in the requirements of a plethora of external commandments in order to assert motives of a profoundly compelling character'. Yet 'these had no power to act as the leaven of all behaviour in penetrating, moulding and organising the multiplicity of commandments and prohibitions'.[16] If the meaning here is not quite clear, it is made obvious enough that Pharisaism was doomed to failure.

Since Martin Metzger's work is regularly consulted by students, his definition of the Pharisees is particularly important: 'For the Pharisees the main requirements were segregation from everything unclean and pagan and meticulous fulfilment of the law ... They approved the oral tradition and interpretation of the scribes ... who strove with the aid of allegorical and casuistic interpretation of Scripture to bring all spheres of life under the legal system.'[17] Jesus' 'criticism of casuistry and legalism was bound to provoke the opposition of the Pharisees'.[18] In Jesus' supreme commandment of love the Pharisees saw 'only unpardonable infringement of the law'. His claim to act and speak with divine authority was something 'the Pharisees could regard only as presumption and blasphemy, and they therefore demanded his death'.[19]

The Pharisees are described similarly in the work of Leipoldt/Grundmann: 'Pride in having fulfilled the law leads to merciless condemnation of sinners and to overweening arrogance. The rabbis are particularly noted for their self-confidence, which leads them to demand the greatest respect in public.'[20] But this does not prevent them from constantly oscillating between arrogance and profound despondency, particularly when death is imminent. But in the many examples in history of Jewish martyrs—Rabbi Akiba, for instance, in A.D. 135—there is no evidence of arrogance or despondency. As far as the gospel tradition is concerned, there is 'no doubt that the conflict of Jesus with his [Pharisee] opponents, which became particularly fierce and finally cost him his life, arose from the fact that they opposed ... his attitude of mercy. His indifference to their style of observing the law provided them with an excuse for bringing a charge against him and keeping him under surveillance until they could draw the net tight and bring him to his death.'[21] We shall have to return in the next chapter in greater detail to this claim that the Pharisees were guilty of the death of Jesus.

Günther Schiwy also refers to the Pharisees in a description of conditions at the time of Jesus. On Matthew 1.1–17 he explains: 'The theological significance of the genealogy seems to be that the Jewish Christians, despite all subtle or violent molestations on the part of the Pharisees and the Synagogue under their influence, should not allow themselves to be distracted from the fact that in Jesus the promise of the Messiah given to Abraham has been fulfilled and thus too the mission of the Jewish people has become clear: to bear witness to Jesus.'[22] This really seems to impose a preconceived interpretation on the text, so that we might speak here too of 'subtlety'. The charges against the Pharisees and scribes are sharply formulated: 'Only when the scribes created a "tradition of the elders" by artificial and exaggerated interpretation of the Mosaic law and declared the tradition to be more important than the written law, only when the Pharisees claimed to fulfil the law by their own efforts and as their own achievements and extolled such achievements as the only way to salvation: only then was the average devout person unable to find his way through the clauses of the law, while the pharisaic "devout" person deceived himself and lost sight of God himself behind the law.'[23] 'Through hair-splitting which they made profitable, through pride in regard to the less knowledgeable, through hypocritical legalistic piety and inordinate ambition, they [the scribes] in the eyes of Jesus had misused their function of leadership.'[24] 'If the teachers of the proselytes are themselves hypocrites and have a mentality which leads to hell, how much more their Gentile disciples.'[25] On Matthew 23.23–6: 'Jesus again unmasks the mendacity of the "righteous" who *rob* the poor even of their last penny for their legal advice.'[26] He then quotes the apocryphal (first-century) 'Assumption of Moses', 7–410, where the latter is shown the transgressors of the law in hell, who are identified with the Pharisees.

Bo Reicke briefly sums up his judgement: 'In scrupulous detail the Pharisees analyzed and discussed the books of the Bible, which provided the legal norm ... This exegetical discussion was called "midrash" ... Among the Pharisees, the biblical material furnishing the legal norm was supplemented more and more, and eventually almost replaced, by the exegetical tradition itself, the "tradition of the elders" ... For different reasons, the Sadducees ... and Jesus himself ... reacted against certain tendencies to relativize the Scriptures and prefer traditions or authorities.'[27] 'To a modern reader, their crabbed and casuistic pedantry will no doubt seem capriciously Oriental.'[28] Reicke calls Paul a 'Pharisaic lay brother'.[29] Their teaching was related to a 'strict observance of cultic purity'. To the Pharisees 'God had revealed the norms of purity through holy scriptures, traditions and scribes ... To preserve and develop the purity of this Levitical covenant people, the scribes had to master and interpret the commandments and statutes exactly ...'.[30] Here, as also in Jeremias' book, *Jerusalem in the Time of Jesus*, the Pharisees are regarded as a closed community very similar to the Qumran sect, for whom the ethical consequences of the covenant with God were less important than the merely external regulations of purity.

For Romano Guardini also, the grounds for Jesus' criticism of the Pharisees and scribes are 'usually ritualistic'.[31] 'The real reason, however, lies deeper. Jesus' opponents feel that here is a will foreign to their own. What they desire is the perpetuance of the old covenant ... When they notice that the new Rabbi mentions neither the temple nor the Kingdom of Israel; that he questions the world and the value of earthly existence ... they feel that he is an alien spirit and cannot rest until they have him safely under ground. So much for the Pharisees, the strictly orthodox, nationalistic "conservatives".'[32] But Guardini omits to mention that the Pharisees just are not purely nationalistic and in particular, in their interpretation of Scripture, are not conservative but often almost revolutionary and want to adapt the law to the situation of their own time.

In his widely read book, *Jerusalem in the Time of Jesus*, Joachim Jeremias seems to start out from two unproved and very debatable arguments. In the first place he regards the scribes as authors not only of the oral tradition, but also of the apocalyptic writings: according to him, Talmud and apocalyptic belong to the same school and are taught by the same Rabbis, the Talmud publicly, the apocalyptic cosmology, which he calls ' "esoteric" midrash and "esoteric" haggadah', secretly. Without entering here into the false opposition between *midrash* and *haggadah*—the opposite of *haggadah* is *halakah* and both are *midrash*—it need only be stressed that most scholars, as opposed to Jeremias (who uses Schlatter's arguments), do not regard the Rabbis as authors of the apocalyptic writings; on the contrary, their attitude to apocalyptic can be described as downright hostile. Hence his conclusion is at least dubious if not simply false: 'We understand therefore that the scribes were venerated, like the prophets of old, with unbounded respect and reverential awe, as bearers and teachers of sacred esoteric knowledge; their words had sovereign authority.'[33] In addition to Schlatter, his sources are the out-dated works of Strack/Billerbeck, Wellhausen, and Eduard Meyer.

His second, totally unproved assertion makes the Pharisees a rigidly isolated group, organized according to strict rules— they form 'closed communities'[34]—and he defines them in terms adapted to the Qumran sect and drawn from the writings of the latter. Qumran serves as a model in his arguments, and he applies the regulations and norms valid there to the much more loosely organized Pharisaic groups. Whatever he has to say about the organization and membership of the Pharisees and scribes does not seem to agree with what is otherwise known about them. For instance: 'The priests took part to a great extent in the Pharisaic movement, and this is explained by the fact that this movement had its origin in the Temple. It sought to raise to the level of a general norm the practice of purity laws even among non-priestly folk, those laws which need only be enforced for priests when they ate the heave-offering.'[35] He admits that they were 'earnest and self-sacrificing; but all too often they were not free from uncharitableness and pride with regard to the masses ... who did not observe the demands of religious laws as they did, and in contrast to whom the Pharisees considered themselves to be the true Israel'.[36] 'According to the Fourth Gospel, the condemnation of Jesus was the work of the Pharisees.'[37] Jeremias adds, however, immediately: 'but this can scarcely be true'. In fact, in connection with the trial itself the Pharisees are mentioned only incidentally (John 11.57; 18.3). The latter must be the result of an editorial error, for the

Pharisees had no 'officers' whom they could have sent to arrest Jesus.

According to Jeremias the Pharisees were the uncrowned rulers of Israel: 'There is something very impressive about the way in which the people unreservedly followed the Pharisees. For the Pharisees fought on two fronts; not only did they oppose the Sadducees, but as the true Israel they drew a hard line between themselves and the masses ... This opposition grew to the dimensions of a caste distinction on the part of the Pharisees.'[38] There is a contradiction here. Why should the 'masses' follow unreservedly the very men who had set themselves apart from them and who even despised them? On the contrary, the Pharisees were small people who led their devout lives in the midst of the masses and did not—like the Qumran sect—regard themselves alone as the 'true Israel'.

In his *Geschichte Jesu Christi* Walter Grundmann stresses the unbridgeable opposition between Jesus' message and Pharisaism: 'A decision must be made between brotherliness and selfish fear of being placed at a disadvantage, between joy in sonship and brotherhood and harsh, joyless service.'[39] As an example of the attitude of the Pharisees he makes use of the end of the parable of the Prodigal Son (Luke 15.25–32): 'The figure of the elder son becomes perceptible already in the way they deny themselves the common joy of brotherliness and stick to their joyless service, because of selfish fear for their merit; thus their righteousness becomes ... dubious and threatens to become unrighteousness.'[40] The author has explained the parable in the way that suits his general scheme; according to this, Christianity contains a call to brotherliness which was neither known nor practised previously. It is an arbitrary interpretation to see the Pharisee in the elder brother. But he goes on further: 'The Gospel tradition makes known the clear opposition of Jesus to Pharisaism. And it leaves scarcely any doubt of the fact that the conflict was sparked off by Jesus' fraternal behaviour towards those who were despised by the Pharisees and by the way he offered them access to the kingdom of God. From all this there emerged an opposition which reached into the depths and ended—historically speaking—with Jesus' crucifixion.'[41] This is the dawn of God's kingdom, and the Pharisees set themselves against it 'and against everything that follows from it and questions their position'.[42] The opposition between Jesus and the Pharisees is made so acute here that it becomes the reason for his death.

Regardless of form- or redaction-criticism or of the historical situation in which the Gospel was composed, Grundmann interprets Matthew—especially Chapters 6 and 23—as typical for Jesus' attitude to the Pharisees: 'The men whose ostentatious piety Jesus attacks ... are called hypocrites, and they are assured that they have had their reward, since they were seen. They have nothing more therefore to expect from God. The word "hypocrite" is certainly used to suggest that they are like actors putting on a show of piety. It characterizes them as people whose worship of God is false, people who can be subjectively sincere but who are lost in the sight of God. Thus it becomes clear that a break has come in the struggle with Pharisaism. Jesus separates his disciples from them, calls them hypocrites, and pronounces God's judgement that they have nothing more to expect from him.'[43] A separate study would be required to decide how far this 'separation' is historically accurate. Many New Testament scholars would admit that the break must be seen as coming much later, six decades after the death of Jesus, at the time of the definitive redaction of Matthew, and that motives other than 'lack of brotherliness' or 'hypocrisy' played a part in it. But Grundmann is quite certain of his position: 'He perceives that the Pharisees rely on themselves; therefore their piety remains merely play-acting and not an encounter with God, since he does not respond to this display of their piety.'[44] Did it never occur to the author that it is somewhat foolhardy to think that he can so scrutinize the nature of divinity, that he can interpret so precisely God's judgement on a group of men? How does this square with 'brotherliness'?

Almost all authors make the same kind of judgement on the Pharisees, the emphasis varying only slightly in the light of a particular time or ideology: 'They were the true champions of that technique of piety whose constant concern it was at every step of their life to fulfil some commandment and to violate none.'[45] This is how Martin Dibelius puts it in his popular book, *Jesus*. But is it so wrong—following also the Gospel accounts and especially the first and second Letter of John—to fulfil the commandments and not to transgress any of them? Is it not, on the other hand, the sole proof which man can give in this world of his real love for God? But for Dibelius the essential thing is to bring out the absolute opposition of Jesus' message to the teaching of the Pharisees: 'A kind of preaching [like that of Jesus] that is concerned so exclusively with what is coming in the future must stand in sharpest contrast to a system that is built on a give-and-take between God and man in the present. To be sure, the strictest representatives of Jewish piety, the Pharisees, also "believed" in the coming Messiah and his Kingdom, but . . . they were satisfied with the present. They believed themselves to be square with God, as the Pharisee voices it in the parable (Luke 18.11). The devaluation of those duties through the principle that "one thing is necessary" must have appeared to them as threatening to undermine and ruin the whole system of piety.'[46] What Jewish 'devout' person— the Pharisee in this case—would ever have thought he had rendered to God all his due or that he was 'square with God'?

In a later chapter there will be more to be said about the Anglo-American portrayal of Judaism and how it compares with the traditional presentation on the Continent. But at this point it may be of interest to quote Paul Tillich, who has taught both in Germany and in America. His opinion on the conflict between Jesus and the Pharisees is far more discriminating. Under the heading, 'The New Being in Jesus as the Christ as the Conquest of Estrangement', he explains that there is no absolute guilt. 'The Pharisees were the pious ones of their time, and they represented the law of God, the preparatory revelation, without which the final revelation could not have happened. If Christians deny the tragic element in the encounter between Jesus and the Jews . . . they are guilty of a profound injustice. And this injustice early produced a Christian anti-Judaism which is one of the permanent sources of modern anti-Semitism. It is regrettable that even today much Christian instruction is consciously or unconsciously responsible for this kind of anti-

Jewish feeling. This can be changed only if we frankly admit that the conflict between Jesus and his enemies was a tragic one.'[47] Although even here there is no objective portrayal of the Pharisees and although here too the historical situation is not mentioned, the conflict is described less one-sidedly and in a less biased way by this German-American.

This may be compared with what Ethelbert Stauffer has to say about Pharisees and scribes in his widely read *New Testament Theology*: 'The Pharisees encompass sea and land to make one new convert to the people of the law.' Despite his quotations from the Gospel, Stauffer here exaggerates the proselytizing zeal of the Pharisees at that time. He continues: 'But all they do is to make a son of hell out of him (Matt. 23.15). For the instruction given by the Synagogue suffers from the fatal contradiction between teaching and life.'[48] Immediately after this he brings in the parable of the Pharisee and the publican at prayer. The Pharisee 'no longer has his delight in God, but in his own piety'. This is the worst 'form of pious self-gratification (Luke 18.9; cf. Matt. 23.6f.). People of this sort have all they want. There is but one thing lacking—the approval of God (Luke 18.14). But Jesus does not just watch the Pharisees from a distance when they stand and pray (Luke 20.47). He knows what is inside a man (Mark 2.8; John 2.25) and he calls the legally righteous "whited sepulchres" (Matt. 23.27). A thin covering of righteousness hides what is really a grave full of death and decay ... The contradiction between teaching and life is a mere nothing compared with this conflict between the inner and the outer which is particularly widespread in those who take the law literally (Matt. 23.25ff.; cf. Mark 7.6). Jesus calls them hypocrites and sons of hell (Matt. 23.15). What Jesus sees at work at this point is the deep mediocrity of the adversary.'[49]

The conflict is unavoidable and inexcusable. Jesus fights against the scribes' exegesis of the law: 'The scribes and Pharisees and their associates put up a very determined resistance to this encroachment on their preserves.'[50] Paul too proves this: 'His one-time associates thought of themselves as "leaders of the blind". They boast of the law and of their learning in it (Rom. 2.17ff.). But there is little to justify their pride (Rom.

2.5ff; 3.9ff), for their conduct is scandalous.'[51] Jesus himself 'exposed the tension between the inward and the outward for what it really was, whereas the Pharisees could only get more and more involved in it'.[52] The Torah-Jew takes his last stand, he reaches the point of death to which the Torah is bound to lead, since it cannot grant God's righteousness to man. How one-sided and simplified is Stauffer's view of the situation by comparison with that of Tillich! He is content with a literal interpretation of certain New Testament texts, without appealing to history or to Jewish sources.

Unfortunately even so highly qualified a scholar as Günther Bornkamm is guilty of a similar simplification. With the Pharisees and the scribes we find, he says, 'the oddest subtleties of casuistry',[53] and they turn daily life into a burden. It is true that God's radical demand is not unknown to Israel; 'It is, however, typical for the Jews [again the distinction between Israel and the Jews], as we see exemplified in the teaching and attitude of the scribes and Pharisees, that God's will and law are understood in the sense of a legal statute with which one may not argue. A legal statute which fences life in on all sides has also this implication: there are as many gaps in the fence as there are posts.'[54]

If famous exegetes speak in this way, it is not surprising that less well known theologians repeat what they say. Thus Karlmann Beyschlag in *Die Bergpredigt und Franz von Assisi* writes of the ethics of the Pharisees: 'When Jesus openly turns against the Pharisees, he does not condemn them for turning God's will into law, but for turning it into what is wrong and for covering up the wrong with the appearance of piety and of being pleasing to God. What provokes Jesus' anger is not the fact that the Pharisees are legalists at the bottom of their hearts, but that they are hypocrites.'[55]

Nor can we expect any correct estimate of the Pharisees, their teaching, and their role from Leonhard Goppelt's important work, *Christentum und Judentum* (*Jesus, Paul and Judaism*; see Bibliography). 'The indictment against the Pharisees and scribes as it was summed up by the Evangelists reads: "hypocrisy." In them appearance and reality contradicted each other.

The scribes taught God's commandment and the Pharisees zealously tried to put it into practice, but neither obeyed it. What was their disobedience? Jesus ... did make clear that this legalistic idea of fulfilling the Law by doing the works that it commanded was a far cry from what the Law actually demands, especially from that attitude of heart that the Law demands ... And He further insisted that this disobedience of the heart was encouraged rather than exposed by their niggling over fine questions of right and wrong, that it was camouflaged rather than remedied by their zeal. The scribes, in their exegesis of the Law, were concerned to determine its boundaries precisely so as to minimize the risk of violating it. But in actuality this helped them to evade it ...'[56] 'Because this scribal interpretation of the Law and the corresponding practice of the Pharisees misused the commandments by making them means of self-assertion before God and man, Jesus shoved this interpretation aside and brought man face to face with God's commandments themselves.'[57] It is debatable whether this is accurate even in the light of Christian theology. Does not Jesus place man directly before his own person as Mediator and does he not demand also as sign of faith and love the fulfilment of his commandments (for example, 2 John 6.8–9, if, like Goppelt, we are to keep to New Testament quotations)?

Goppelt also sees in the parable of the prodigal son 'the most graphic picture of Pharisaic piety imaginable. This is man under the Law! He does indeed keep God's commandments outwardly (Luke 18.10–12; Mark 10.20). But he does so as a slave obeys his master—not out of love but for the sake of reward. And what a reward! Just to make merry with his friends!'[58] Quite apart from the style, exclamation marks, and queries, this is a forced, allegorical exegesis. 'The Pharisee ... did not love God, and therefore he could not love his brother ... Since the righteous brother wanted to be rewarded for his accomplishments, he was naturally angry at his father's goodness toward the prodigal (Luke 15.28; Matt. 20.15). In just the same way, the completely egocentric, slavish attitude of the righteous Pharisees toward God and their lovelessness toward their neighbors became glaringly evident when they protested against

Jesus' saving of sinners. In their attitude the Pharisees took a position at the opposite pole from the God who desires "mercy and not sacrifice".[59] Can this statement be accepted without more ado? Was it not a Jew who wrote Psalm 51: 'Thou hast no delight in sacrifice; were I to give a burnt offering, thou wouldst not be pleased. The sacrifice acceptable to God is a broken spirit; a broken and contrite heart, O God, thou wilt not despise'? And have not Pharisaic Jews both in Jesus' time and until today recited this psalm in prayer?

We may quote again Martin Dibelius' clear condemnation of the Pharisees: 'The judgment of the Gospel is directed above all against the Pharisees, against those who make a claim upon God before others based on the pre-eminence of pious behaviour. Their righteousness ... entitled them to no such claim. They can even become ensnared in sin by their scrupulous technique in fulfilling the law, because they forget the big things in order to perform the small ones. But when Jesus describes all of them together as hypocrites he does so ... because they do not understand their position in the sight of God. Because they, like the Pharisee in the parable, approach God in a spirit of pre-eminence which is perhaps quite commendable among men, as though their "righteousness" were also righteousness in his sight. Because they do not see that the only thing befitting a man in God's sight is the publican's prayer: God be merciful to me, a sinner.'[60]

Martin Dibelius is quite certain that they do not see this. We may wonder if he has ever read the *Selihot*, the penitential prayers before the New Year and the Day of Atonement, which in sum simply amount to the appeal: God forgive me and be merciful to me, a sinner.

In an article on Matthew 23 Ernest Haenchen has to cope with the question of Pharisaism. He really does attempt to do justice to the political situation at the time of the redaction of this Gospel. So he distinguishes quite correctly between the judgement of Matthew, for whom rabbinate and Pharisaism are 'one whole mass of perdition',[61] and the judgement of Jesus himself. But Jesus, too, sharply criticized the Pharisees, as is evident from the parable of the publican and the Pharisee. The latter 'is not a hypocrite ... The very fact, however, that he is not pretending, but has a good conscience when he thinks he is at peace with God: it is just this which is so terrible and which excludes him from fellowship with God.'[62] These 'moralists' in particular were Jesus' opponents. By his attempt to stress the moral quality of Pharisaism and yet to present these men as Jesus' arch-enemies, Haenchen—it seems—goes a step further in his interpretation of their condemnation by Jesus: 'Jesus is convinced that this Pharisee knows nothing of the true God. He does not know him at all ... he has never heard his voice. But the publican has perceived it ... [he] has discovered the God of love, whose heart is greater than our heart. What does the Pharisee know of this God? If we are not afraid to use a harsh expression for what Jesus describes here, we can say that Jesus and the Pharisee are simply not talking about the same God. Therefore Jesus' preaching and Jesus' action amount to an attack directed at the heart of Pharisaism and threatening to destroy it: the image of God which the Pharisee —without hypocrisy—truly venerates. This is the reason why Jesus' attack was felt by the Pharisees to be a dire threat and provoked their deadly enmity.'[63] The charge made here against the Pharisees goes much deeper than the usual one of hypocrisy: they do not even pray to the same God as Jesus and the Christians; their God is a false God. This position is very close to that of Marcion or to that of Harnack, his biographer: Judaism's idea of God is different from that of Christianity and can consequently be regarded, with the Old Testament as a whole, as finished and obsolete. One might almost prefer the charge of hypocrisy to the judgement pronounced here: Jesus 'pronounced judgement on him [the Pharisee] because it was precisely the consistent, strict, and devout Pharisee who obscured and distorted the true image of God; because this very Pharisee—in striving to be obedient to God—in fact turned away from God and not towards him'.[64] A more radical condemnation—and distortion—of true Pharisaism is scarcely possible.

Bousset and Gressmann adopt a singular method. Occasion- ally they say or quote something good about the Pharisees, only to withdraw or devalue it immediately. Thus *Berakhoth* (F.17a) is quoted: 'One may do much or little; it is all one provided he directs his heart to heaven.'[65] But sayings like this are quickly forgotten: 'The main trend of Pharisaic morality is however correctly described by Jesus.'[66] 'Despite their singularity, there is something touching and even impressive' about Hillel, Gamaliel, and Jochanan. 'But the reverse side cannot be forgotten. What a narrow world has religion become here! All independent, intellectual alertness and freshness, life itself, reduced to death. One of the greatest things about Jesus was his opposition to these *grammateis* ... that he saved the people —at least for a time—from the theologians.'[67] We might add that it is also high time for us today to be saved from the anti-Jewish tradition of Bousset and Gressman and their colleagues.

Bousset and Gressmann also shared the view of many theologians that the Pharisees exercised a strict, arbitrary rule over the people. Pharisees and scribes then had 'the reins in their hands. They led the people, they forced even the priestly aristocracy into their service.'[68] The people followed them blindly, but the Pharisees 'looked down on them with lofty arrogance'.[69] At first the Pharisees had been the party of the progressives, but 'when they had gained power, they very quickly became the conservatives, the bearers of a rigid piety'.[70] A little later, after unwillingly making some concessions: 'The reverse side is evident: the self-satisfied certainty unaware of any questions and problems, the narrow-minded isolation and over-weening pride permitting no other style to count ... condemnation and judgement, spying and watching, overlooking their own weakness ... the complete incapacity to understand the time and the world around them'.[71] There is a typical addition to this in a footnote: 'This judgement is not rendered erroneous just because we can quote a saying of Hillel: "Judge not thy fellow until thou art come to his place" (*Aboth* i, 4). A single saying like this could hardly be heard as long as there was no decision to abandon this whole system of piety.'[72] The charge that the Pharisees were incapable of understanding their world and time is so completely unjustified that one example may suffice to refute it. Rabbi Jochanan ben Zakai understood so well what would be the consequences of war against Rome that he got away in good time from the doomed city of Jerusalem, in order to set up a new centre where the life and faith of the covenant people could be preserved away from the temple and capital set for destruction.

Bousset and Gressmann indicate their sources: these are the non-rabbinical apocalyptic writings. They use traditional Jewish sources only at second hand, usually from Ferdinand Weber's *System der altsynagogalen palästinensischen Theologie* (1880), of which G. F. Moore said as early as 1921 that it applied the system of Protestant theology to Judaism and regarded legalism as the essence of the Jewish religion. 'The motive and method of the volume are in fact apologetic throughout; the author, like so many of his predecessors, sets himself to prove the superiority of Christianity to Judaism.'[73] Although any scholar now would admit that little reliance can be placed on Weber, a book like that of Bousset/Gressmann—using this kind of source—is regarded even today as an introduction to Judaism at the time of Christ which can be recommended.

The influential Adolf Schlatter is a severe critic and goes into detail: washing is not important in itself, but it is typical of Pharisaism. Jesus 'refused to obey the Pharisaic tradition, since it involved a transgression of the divine commandment'. He rejected the tradition 'since it comprised propositions commanding sin'.[74] The example given is the *qorban* already mentioned, which is certainly not a customary pretext in Judaism for taking an oath freeing a person from his obligation of providing due support for his parents. It would be too complicated to go into detail here on the question of oaths. But it may be recalled that in the *Mishnah* Rabbi Meir envisages the situation of a man who has made a vow without realizing that it would involve offending against love of neighbour and other commandments: if he then says, ' "Had I known that this was so, I would not have made the vow", he may be released from his vow' (*Nedarim* 9.4). This seems to have been the general practice.

The Pharisees were intent only on external purity, not on

that 'which comes from the heart ... compulsive washing [turned] attention away from this and set up instead a fabricated purity.'[75] Jesus rejected Pharisaism in its totality: 'He called it sin when the Pharisee combined with piety arrogant self-esteem and harshness towards men.... The Pharisee discredits the penitent and light-heartedly condemns the innocent ... Undisciplined cultivation of wild, sensual lust was easily attached to pride.'[76] As evidence of this he quotes Matthew 12.39 ('an evil and adulterous generation seeks for a sign'): an example of what can be read into the Gospels if one sets one's mind to it.

The scribes are no better off: 'They forced the congregation to continual prayer and were incapable of praying themselves ... they bound themselves daily to love God with all their strength and constantly paraded their vanity; they demanded the preservation of immaculate purity and did not see what made them unclean.'[77] The Pharisaic way of life is involved in an abominable contradiction: 'It combines doing what is right with sin. On the one hand was the great punctiliousness with which the Pharisee practised his duty in regard to tithes, on the other the open struggle against the essential reality of the law, against judgement, goodness, and fidelity; on the one hand the concern for purity and on the other the crude impurity of their feasting; on the one hand their burning missionary zeal and on the other the mischief to which they incited those who fell into their hands.... To Pharisaic piety the coupling of righteousness and sin, obedience and disobedience, did not seem abnormal.'[78] On the contrary, the one justified the other, 'and therefore Jesus saw in Pharisaism the sin that was fatal to Jewry'.[79] It is scarcely an exaggeration to see at work here the influence of the wide-spread German anti-Semitism of the twenties, making it impossible for the author to judge the Judaism of the first century objectively; there is no trace here of any consultation of sources outside the Gospels.

Eduard Meyer begins his study on the Pharisees with texts from the Church Fathers and from Schürer on their 'casuistry' and 'sophistry'.[80] The scribes 'parade their correctness and purity ostentatiously and are able to make use of their position as pastors of souls for material exploitation especially of widows (Mark 12.38–40)'.[81] The observance of the law is totally separated from all truly religious factors, such as covenant and election. It is always a question of 'devising precepts of purity, of trifling regulations, which are highly appropriate for denouncing opponents and exciting the masses ... but are without any intrinsic value ... The masses run to the Pharisees and are disconcerted when someone like Jesus ventures to reject their precepts as human innovations.'[82] For Meyer even Paul remains a Pharisee and uses the Pharisaic method of Scripture interpretation. Through allegorizing, 'fantastic combinations with views which are quite strange to him', Paul achieves 'the most violent reinterpretations'.[83] In this way Paul changes the simple, unerring word of God.

It is not surprising to find that Julius Wellhausen belongs to this tradition: 'The Pharisees were past masters of piety'[84] and looked down proudly on the ignorant. We can only continue to wonder how these despised 'ignorant' people allowed themselves to be so dominated by the Pharisees. The scribes too pursued 'the old trend ... to bring the whole of life under the sacred rule ... The result was a spiritual servitude more effective than any that has ever existed. The congregations submitted willingly to the new hierarchy, the nomocracy of the scribes.'[85] 'The scribes and Pharisees did not want to do good, but to protect themselves from sin; their observation of conventional regulations was no good to anyone and was pleasing neither to God nor to man.' Jesus 'rejects the sublime goodness which devours the houses of widows ... which conspires in God's honour against fulfilling a child's duty to mother and father'.[86] As far as this rejection of the child's duty to parents is concerned, we may quote a passage from the Jerusalem Talmud (*Kiddushin* i.9) where it is said that the transgression of a number of precepts may be forgiven in view of good deeds which count against it, but any reward is excluded as a result of transgressing one precept, the failure to honour father and mother.

Emil Schürer quotes *Aboth* i, 3: 'Be not like slaves that minister to the master for the sake of receiving a bounty, but be like slaves that minister to the master not for the sake of receiving a bounty.' This is all very fine, but he adds: 'It is by no means a correct expression of the basic sentiment of Pharisaic Judaism. This is in fact the mood of servants who minister for the sake of the reward.'[87]

Is it ironical to remark how odd it is for someone who knows the Jewish sources only at second hand to claim to judge more correctly than the Pharisaic Jew himself 'the basic sentiment of Pharisaic Judaism'? Would a Christian regard the opinion of a Buddhist on the essence of Christianity as binding and justified, especially if the Buddhist could scarcely find his way among the original texts? And yet Schürer's portrayal of Judaism has been taken as authoritative even up to the present time. From 1902 till 1976 there has been no perceptible difference in the judgement—or, more precisely in the condemnation—of Pharisaism.

Schürer also speaks of the industry of the Pharisaic scribes: 'They have broken down the law into many thousands of individual precepts.' This was really their most serious fault, for 'all free, moral action is now completely crushed by the burden of particular statutory requirements ... At every moment of life people act not in virtue of internal motives, not in freely giving effect to a moral disposition, but under the external constraint of a statutory requirement.' Small things and great are of equal weight, 'and at the same time there is of course no higher task than to do justice to the letter for the sake of the letter. The important thing is not the internal disposition, but the external correctness of the act.'[88]

Finally we may cite once again some examples from the work of French biblical scholars who entirely agree with the German writers and are certainly also typical for the Italian and Spanish tradition. In French biblical scholarship M.-J. Lagrange had an authority even greater than that of Schürer in German. In 1908 he wrote: 'In its totality [the teaching of the scribes] is forced, over-subtle, arbitrary, and artificial. It would be seriously derogatory to Roman law—reason in writing—to compare it with the Talmud. We know the tree by its fruits.'[89] He concludes from the fine, conciliatory saying of the Rabbis on the

need sometimes of compromise for the sake of peace, that this
means 'deliberate dissimulation.'[90] Then follows the inevitably
one-sided comparison of Christian and Jewish attitudes: 'We
have often heard Israel clamorously confessing its faults to God;
but it has a greater repugnance to admit being in the wrong
before men. A Christian does not hesitate to admit the faults
of his clergy; in the eyes of devout Jews the Rabbis have always
been irreproachable. But, not being able constantly to rise above
the limitations of human nature, they adopted a mask.'[91] The
first statement is certainly true with reference to a pope such
as Alexander VI, whose 'faults' were displayed on the world-
stage; but when has the average Christian been ready publicly
to admit and to castigate the faults and abuses of the clergy
and the hierarchy? And, on the other hand, how often have
Jewish congregations quite publicly argued with their Rabbis
and even dismissed them without more ado when they were
not up to their task?

But we find something even better in Lagrange's much later
work, *Le Judaisme avant Jésus-Christ*. 'We think ... that the
gospel portrays a Pharisee of the most dangerous type ... He
is a hypocrite, for he pretends to be living among the saints
... and, according to the custom of his sect, he quotes the law,
but only in order to deceive ... our man carefully conceals his
luxurious life: after nights of debauchery he presents himself
behind the smiling mask of innocence.' Where did Lagrange
get all this from? The Gospels? Or could it have been from
Edouard Drumont, the notorious anti-Semitic author of the
Dreyfus period? But let us hear Lagrange again. It reads like
a detective novel: 'He [the Pharisee] gets into a house and, like
a serpent, tries to seduce the innocent with his cunning words.
When he has undermined one house, he passes to another and
pursues his secret intrigues, insatiable as Hades.'[92]

He defines the Pharisees as people who flattered themselves
that they knew God's laws and their application better than
any of the others and imposed these as a burden on the nation.
The main fault of the Pharisees consisted in 'making religious
zeal a reason for avoiding cordial relations with their neighbours
and almost a duty to despise them as impure'.[93] He compares

the Catholic religious orders with the Pharisaic communities and sees the fundamental difference to lie in the fact that the orders have the task of spreading love for God and neighbour, while the aristocratic Pharisee binds himself to avoid even buying vegetables from the peasants, the *'am ha-arez*. This sounds like a joke, but Lagrange means it quite seriously.

The scribes are slaves to the letter of Scripture, but on the other hand they interpret the laws just as they fancy in each particular case: 'The relentlessness of the Rabbis in demanding the literal fulfilment of all the details descriptive of the messianic period, details which they exaggerated to the point of absurdity, is what mainly distinguishes their method from that of the apostles. It is one of the most serious obstacles holding them back from Christianity.'[94] This statement contains at least two mistakes. The Rabbis did not give any detailed description of the coming of the Messiah; this was left to the Qumran sect. But, secondly, the evangelists did seek out carefully all those texts of Scripture which point to Jesus as Messiah and this with a one-sidedness which is generally admitted today.

The work of Joseph Bonsirven, *On the Ruins of the Temple*, which appeared in French about the same time (1928), merely repeats what we have read in other authors. The Pharisees 'sought to save as much of the Torah as possible by a still more bitter exclusiveness; they surrounded the Law and the chosen people with manifold and thorny hedges, they strengthened the sectarian observances and aggravated the precepts; the walls of the Temple had crumbled, and in revenge they erected the sombre ramparts of the Ghetto.'[95]

The well-known modern New Testament scholar, Pierre Benoit, was mentioned in the last chapter in connection with his negative view of the law. In his essays (for example, 'The Law and the Cross according to St Paul') he certainly has in mind the Pharisees, but mentions them merely incidentally as former associates of Paul. Thus in a footnote: 'It is quite certain in any case that the great majority of his co-religionists rested happily and proudly on this Law which they flattered themselves they kept well enough, the goodness of which they were never tired of praising and which they thought of chiefly in its flattering aspect of a national privilege' (with a reference to Bon-sirven).[96] In a short chapter on 'Rabbi Akiba Ben Joseph' he stresses particularly the great hatred between the scribes and the simple people, referring to Strack/Billerbeck: 'If we recall the disdainful contempt with which the Pharisees and other scrupulous observers of the law regarded the ordinary people and considered contact with them to be impure, we shall under-stand the hatred with which the latter paid them back.'[97] Despite this contempt, it is nevertheless notable that, according to all the authors, the mass of the people ran after the Pharisees and not only obeyed them and the scribes, but surrounded them with deep respect. Akiba himself, of whom Benoit writes here, had formerly been an *'am ha-arez*, one of the simple people, but had only one ideal which he was finally able to realize at the age of forty: to become a scribe. He sacrificed everything to this ideal and became one of the greatest authorities on the law, and for this he died as a martyr with the words of the law on his lips.

In closing we need only add that the image and work of the Pharisees and scribes as they emerge from these excerpts from typical theological works of the last decades are drawn almost exclusively from the New Testament. But there was no intention in the New Testament—and this must be constantly stressed—of giving an objective historical presentation, a 'contemporary history' of the first century and of the people living at that time. The New Testament is proclamation, *kerygma* of the person of Jesus as the risen *Kyrios*. The writings of the New Testament emerged at different times, but all of them after the controversy between the early Church and Judaism had already become acute. This conflict is reflected in almost all the books of the New Testament. To attempt to understand Pharisees and scribes solely in the light of the New Testament is the same thing—*mutatis mutandis*—as to put together an image of Jesus from the talmudic sources and to regard this as historically true. A committed faith in Jesus as the Christ and as founder of the Church should not prevent us from studying, recognizing, and respecting the true nature of Pharisaism. This is possible how-ever only by drawing also on Jewish literature and considering it as an authentic source. Nor can the Judaism of the last nineteen hundred years, which emerged from Pharisaism, be excluded. Faith in Jesus as Lord does not compel his supporters to despise the 'others'. On the contrary, it should make the Christian particularly sensitive to the values of the Jewish religion; for the latter is in fact the matrix of Christianity. The authors cited here unfortunately completely fail to show any such sympathetic understanding of the true nature of Pharisaic Judaism.

5

Jewish Guilt in
the Death of Jesus

This chapter deals with the most serious and far-reaching accusation which Christians have made against the Jews from time immemorial right up to the present. 'The Jews crucified Christ' became a commonplace, despite all attempts—even those of the Second Vatican Council—to introduce less sweeping statements and to explain the circumstances at the time. Despite doubts about the historical accuracy of the account of the trial before the Sanhedrin, most theologians continue to maintain their former view of an irreconcilable hostility between Jesus and *the* Jews. This hostility is then seen as leading logically to his death.

Thus Joachim Jeremias, whom no one could accuse of anti-Judaism, mentions as it were incidentally at the beginning of his chapter on the Passion that the question of Jesus' death had already been settled after his second transgression of the Sabbath law (Mark 3.6).[1] The death sentence could have been carried out without difficulty in Galilee under the jurisdiction of Herod Antipas. It is surprising that so great an expert on the New Testament does not see here the hand of the redactor, whose theology is partly based on the conflict of Jesus with his opponents from the beginning of his activity to its end, completely regardless of any historical–chronological order.

In the following paragraphs the same author explains: 'Above all, when Jesus decided to carry out the cleansing of the temple, he must have been clear that he was risking his life; and that was in fact the occasion for the definitive official action against him.'[2] We may wonder whether we are reading one of the best-known exegetes of modern times or the Oberammergau Passion Play, where the whole action is in fact initiated by the conflict between Jesus and the sellers and priests in the temple. We may leave aside the question of how far the temple-cleansing was symbolical or historical. In any case in John (2.13–17), who is better informed than the synoptists about Jesus' visits to Jerusalem, it introduces the beginning of his public appearances. In none of the Gospels is it mentioned as a charge in the trial of Jesus before the Sanhedrin. Nor do the offences against the Sabbath represent an action deserving death. They are not among the charges against him, although witnesses of them could easily have been found.

In the discussion on Jesus' prediction of his death, Jeremias also adds as it were incidentally: 'The disciples were spared at Jesus' arrest; in a remarkable way the Jewish authorities were satisfied with the killing of Jesus and left the disciples unmolested.'[3]

In a summary at the end of his famous book, *The Trial of Jesus*, which appeared in its fourth German edition in 1969, Josef Blinzler claims that we would be bound today to come to the same conclusion as the early Christian preachers did about the historical Jewish responsibility: 'The main responsibility rests on the Jewish side.'[4] Whether the sanhedrists were convinced of Jesus' legal guilt or not is impossible to decide. 'When the whole or almost the whole of the Sanhedrin voted for a verdict of guilty, one must conclude that the judges were strongly biased against the Accused. But it is only in the further course of events that the malicious attitude of the sanhedrists emerges quite clearly. They brought an action against Jesus before the Roman governor, charging him with calling himself King of the Jews ... This charge was ... a deliberate distortion of the charge on which their own condemnation had been based. Being aware than they could achieve nothing with the simple charge of blasphemy before the governor's court, they lent his charge a political significance.... The fact that his enemies were not concerned for the law, nor even for a false concept of the law, but were only aiming at the destruction of Jesus at any price, is clear from their efforts to hinder Pilate from pronouncing a free and legal judgment by intimidating him with threats and so forcing him to pass sentence of death.'[5]

'The Jews who incurred this guilt consisted of two groups—the members of the Sanhedrin and the crowds.'[6] Blinzler explains the reasons for this: 'In the first place, the Jewish leaders saw in the popularity of Jesus a danger for their own authority with the populace.' The Sadducees, secondly, feared a Roman intervention. 'Thirdly, the peculiar nature of his religious message had made Jesus disliked and hated ... by the scribes and Pharisees. Hence the mortal enmity which the ruling circles cherished toward Jesus had personal, political, national-istic and religious grounds.'[7] He refers to Peter's saying in the Acts of the Apostles that those involved in Jesus' death acted in ignorance (Acts 3.17). 'When the Apostle admits in his preach-ing that the Jews of Jerusalem and their leaders had not known what they were doing, he only means that, had the Jews known that Jesus was the Messiah and Son of God in the true sense, they would not have brought about his destruction; but he does not mean to absolve them from guilt, for their ignorance was a symptom of their unbelief. And unbelief, in face of the "miracles and wonders and signs" experienced, is guilty and sinful according to the teaching of the New Testament.'[8] And again he weighs the guilt of the Jews and Romans, but, with-out exonerating Pilate completely, decides that 'his guilt is less on the whole than that of the Jews'.[9] Like the rest of the authors, Blinzler approaches the trial of Jesus with a preconceived opinion: if a New Testament text does not fit into his scheme, it simply cannot be taken seriously. On the other hand, every-thing that is said to have happened before the Sanhedrin—for example, the question whether Jesus is 'the Son of the Blessed' (Mark 14.61)—is the simple truth. Not only this but Blinzler also penetrates the intimate conscience of the Sanhedrin and knows exactly why they were bound to be prejudiced against Jesus. No attention is paid to the time of the final composition of the Gospels and the historical situation at the time, which played a part in this final redaction.

Georg Fohrer is an Old Testament scholar, but in his *Studien zur alttestamentlichen Theologie und Geschichte* he includes an article on 'Judentrage und Zionismus'. Jesus took up and ful-filled the message of the prophets and the task of Israel. Fohrer concludes from this: 'The Church therefore, without seeking to carry out a mission to the Jews, must draw Judaism's attention to its task which it has hitherto evaded: the Church must teach Jewry to understand the prophets as fully authorized heralds of its task and Jesus as continuing their proclamation and calling the individual Jew to a decision.'[10] Is this not missionary activity? And is it really the business of a German Christian in 1969 to teach Israel to understand its own prophets? Quite apart from taking for granted their 'rejection of Jesus', what arrogance and self-assurance are implied in wanting to 'draw Judaism's attention to its task'. There are Christians then who —after the almost complete failure of Christian teaching to impress the Jews—venture to tell the latter what is their task, instead of first instructing Christians about their own task.

In accordance with his assumptions, Fohrer continues: 'In Jesus' message therefore legal-national Judaism is surmounted, and at the same time there is fulfilled what Judaism really ought to have fulfilled and to which the prophetic proclamation had invited it. Jesus could have saved Judaism from its wrong path and from its rigidity. His rejection led only to the reinforcement of that wrong attitude to life; by rejecting Jesus, Judaism refused to fulfil its divine task.'[11] These are the consequences of the rejection and dismissal of Jesus by the Jewish people: it is following wrong paths, remains stubborn, and has repudiated its divine task. Fohrer stresses particularly this failure to fulfil its task, the result of which is that the Church has the duty of instructing Israel: 'What then is the deeper reason for the terrible sufferings which have constantly afflicted Jewry? They are not simply—as Christians frequently thought—the consequence of rejecting Jesus, still less a punishment for this. . . . These sufferings can be understood at most as the result of the failure of Judaism to perform its task—or of its denial of this task—which itself includes the rejection of Jesus. Nor are the sufferings of Jewry—as Jews frequently think—the consequence of the fulfilment of Israel's divine task, through which it has become the object of mankind's hatred; for Judaism has not in fact fulfilled its task. It suffers indeed on account of that task which still faces it, by which . . . it is marked, which makes it seem like a foreign body in the world: the world for which it was intended to be an example and model, sign and pointer to an existence founded in God, and—by fulfilling its task—a permanent call to decision for God. But Jewry suffers also because it has always failed to seize this task, by understanding it wrongly, refusing to fulfil it, or rejecting it outright, and seeking security instead in the world in its own way.'[12]

There is not a word about the blame attaching also to Christians for the historical suffering of Jewry during the past two thousand years. Their fate is the fault of the Jews themselves and they failed not only by 'rejecting' Jesus, but in their task as a whole. It must appear today as a real scandal to Jews and to many Christians that a distinguished scholar can make light of this suffering and find no other explanation of 'the deeper cause of the terrible sufferings' of Jewry than the Jews themselves. As far as the present author is aware, no one has taken up or attacked Fohrer's thesis except a Swiss Jewish newspaper.

In the third volume of his *Weg ins Neue Testament*, Günther Schiwy also raises the question why 'the majority of the Jews did not find their way to Christ'. Paul gives 'an answer wholly from the standpoint with which he is familiar. The Jews had become so rigidly attached to their righteousness on the basis of good works that they were no longer sufficiently open to salvation solely by faith in Christ; and it is not God, but man's sin that is responsible for their being no longer sufficiently open to salvation by faith in Christ, for the fact that they got into this state.'[13] Following Paul in the Letter to the Romans, he insists: 'Paul has now made it clear that, if the majority of Jews up to now "are ignorant" (10.3) of the sole possible way to salvation, this is not God's fault; even in the Old Testament, in the past of the chosen people, he spoke clearly enough of "justification by faith", so that the Jews' ignorance would be better described as "mistaking" God's intentions and this is culpable; they had grown so fond of a "righteousness from good works" that they finally became blind both to the Old Testament word of God and then also to the New Testament word in Christ. For it is obvious that God spoke clearly enough to the Jews at the time through Christ and still speaks through those authorized by Christ.'[14] He continues with his interpretation of the Letter to the Romans (11.9–10): 'What we now see therefore in the majority of Jews is that blindness in regard to Christ which had been known in advance and announced, and therefore implanted, by God but brought on by the Jews' own fault, which may not be minimized but which also cannot be regarded as beyond God's power to remove.'[15] This is a reference to the Church's expectation that one day all Israel will acknowledge Christ.

Basically there is only a minimal difference between this mode of interpretation and that of the Church Fathers of the first centuries. The latter, like Christians today, were faced by the need to explain why the Jews have not acknowledged Jesus as Messiah. The quest did not lead them to penetrate more deeply into the history of the first century, into Jewish sources and into living, enduring Judaism. It is thought sufficient to speak of 'blindness' as a result of their own fault: for 'God spoke clearly enough to the Jews through Christ'. Just as with the Church Fathers, therefore, it is regarded as a question of obstinacy, of arbitrary, culpable rejection of the Christian message. It is obvious therefore that the young theological student who accepts this explanation must regard himself also as 'authorised', as one who wants to take the bandages from the eyes of the Jews when circumstances permit; that he must in fact regard this—so to speak—as the task of the Churches. There is no mention here of the fact, nor does it seem to these authors either important or possible, that the juxtaposition of Church and Synagogue is open to a different theological explanation. The Christian-Jewish relationship is burdened by a nineteen-hundred-year-old theological tradition from which it cannot get free.

Leonhard Goppelt has very much the same approach in *Christologie und Ethik*: 'The Church can never overlook this sorrowful function [of the Jews] which has made its mark on them. But the Church also, if it takes the gospel seriously, must see in this resistance the obstinacy and guilt which deprive them of salvation.'[16] Israel still lives, but, 'so to speak, on the lower plane of the promise and the law. But they [Jews today] are different from the Israel of the Old Testament, because they not only did not enter on the plane of fulfilment, but are in opposition to it. Against Christ, they remain attached to the covenant with God eschatologically dissolved by Christ.'[17] Nevertheless, he thinks, the Church must enter into conversation with them, always hoping that this will lead to an encounter with Christ. Under these circumstances can we take it badly if so many Jews refuse to enter into this conversation, just because they suspect that the mission to them has become almost an article of faith in Christianity, and they rightly assume that there is an intention behind the dialogue which represents a threat to their independent existence?

Max Metzger does not see the question differently: 'Israel did not listen to God's call, given through Jesus Christ, and refused to see in Jesus the Messiah, the fulfilment of Old Testament promises.'[18] The author stresses here the hostile attitude of Jewry not only in regard to Christ, but also to Christians, as shown in the 'curse' which was included in their prayers. Jesus, the author explains, went to Jerusalem in order there to face the 'representatives of Israel' with their final decision. 'Israel too must prove its election in its response to God's call given through Jesus Christ.' Jesus claimed 'to act and speak with ultimate divine authority. This claim the Pharisees and scribes could regard only as presumption and blasphemy, and they demanded his death. Before the Roman officials they accused him of resistance to the authority of the state.' Israel then did not accept the Saviour, did not recognize what the disciples had learned after the resurrection. 'God's speaking and acting in the history of Israel and through the history of Israel led to him and found its goal in him.'[19] All this is briefly related and with an extreme simplification of a very complicated process. Nothing is said of the endurance of Judaism, which did not find 'its goal' in Jesus. In any case, Israel has not 'proved' itself: faced with a decision, it made the wrong choice and demanded Jesus' death. Without going into details, it can be said that Leipoldt and Grundmann exaggerate and sharpen the conflict between Jesus and 'his opponents' which 'finally cost him his life'.[20]

Günther Schiwy may be quoted again in his earlier first volume: 'Jesus is the Messiah promised by the Old Testament, but the chosen people rejected him and this resulted in the rejection of the nation in salvation history (but not eternally).'[21] In his second volume, on John's Gospel, his statements are more theologically exact: 'From the standpoint of salvation history it seems that this separation of the Church from the Jewish people was necessary if God's self-communication to all men as it occurred in Christ was not to be frustrated. Nevertheless the "must" of salvation history does not give the Christian the right to condemn the Jews outright and to persecute them as "deicides". Every sinful human being—Christian, Jew, or pagan —is guilty of the death of Jesus in the same way.'[22] But this is not what is said in the first volume: 'Mark's account brings out the fact that it was the Jewish people (and not so much Pilate) who decided the death of Jesus.'[23] This clearly fits in with what the author had already said by way of explanation of Matthew 23: 'Jesus turns directly to the spiritual elite of Judaism. Since in salvation history it would have been precisely the task of the religious leaders of Judaism to make man alert to God's demands by authentic exegesis (interpretation) of the Old Testament revelation and thus to prepare Israel for the advent of God in Jesus, the "woe" is so accusing and menacing at the same time.'[24]

A closer exegesis, such as Schiwy demands from the Jewish leaders, would have shown him that nothing in what we call the Old Testament prepares for the advent of 'God in Jesus', that the incarnation was not understood at all in the lifetime of Jesus even by the disciples and after the resurrection only very gradually by Christians. He would have learned that Old Testament texts—notably Isaiah 7.14—were later wrongly translated and applied to Jesus and that only Christians interpret the Old Testament as in any way related to Jesus; that in this case many verses acquire an over-subtle Christian meaning which they did not possess originally. Even today, in the new age which has dawned through Christ for those who believe in

99

him, a whole series of frequently quoted biblical texts has not yet reached its complete fulfilment (we may recall, for instance, Jeremiah 31.31–4).

In his numerous theological works Karl Rahner mentions Judaism only rarely. In a radio series, *Juden, Christen, Deutsche* (1969), he composed an article, 'Bekenntnis zu Jesus Christus', in which he included Jews among 'anonymous Christians': that is, among those who—unconsciously—are already touched by Jesus and act in accordance with his will, even though they are not explicitly aware of this. It is questionable whether this does justice to the role of Judaism in the world, for—as Gregory Baum, another theologian, once said—to be 'anonymous Christians' is the very thing which devout Jews do not want. Rahner can consider Judaism only from the standpoint of Jesus as Messiah, since Jesus became for all the 'finisher of Old Testament salvation history'.[25] But this is just what he does not mean for Judaism. Rahner does not succeed in seeing Judaism impartially in its own self-understanding. In his 'Meditations on St Ignatius' Exercises', published in 1965, his attitude to the Jews as condemning Jesus and bringing about his death is very traditional, even though he speaks of the guilt of all men in the cross of Christ. Thus he writes: 'The Sanhedrin had already condemned him to death before hearing his sworn testimony that he is the Messiah, the Redeemer sent into the world by God, the fulfiller of the law and of history, the Son of the living God—they condemned him even before they heard this, and interpreted his words as blasphemy deserving death. They do not really take his avowal seriously. In fact, they misuse it as a pretext to secure the death penalty ... Jesus is condemned in the name of good order, national pride, the good of the country, truth, belief in Yahweh.'[26]

Against this and subsequent statements, the author's claim that the Sanhedrin mentality continues even in the Church does not really serve to create a balance. The supreme court is still considered representative of the nation in its refusal of God's plan. Rahner goes on, making use of unmistakable expressions: 'The Jews reject him as a scandal to them even in the name of God. We could almost say that a supernatural demonism is exercising its power in the hatred of this people against the true kingdom of God.'[27] It does not help much to add that this attitude can be found also in the Church, that its members can do the same thing 'as the Jewish people did then: they rejected Jesus before Pilate and thus demanded another Messiah more pleasing to them'.[28]

As a book of meditations and not straightforward theology, this work exercises a more subtle influence and disarms criticism of its assertions. Unfortunately Rahner remains wholly within the established tradition, even though he presents the Jew as the type of a mentality that is possible everywhere and at all times. Indeed it is all the easier to see in him the archetype: the Jewish attitude becomes the example *par excellence* of the wrong attitude to Jesus: 'When St Paul says that the crucified Lord is a stumbling block to the Jews, he is thinking primarily of his own contemporaries who opposed Jesus with fanatical hatred.'[29] All those who make up their own image of God are 'like the Jews who rejected Jesus ... A person with the attitude characterized by St Paul as "Jewish" defends "his" God against anything that could shake him loose from his theological concept. Anything different from what "his" God is supposed to be, is so scandalous that he must fight against it with all the fury of religion.'[30]

He repeats: 'The crucified Lord is betrayed and abandoned by his friends, rejected by his people, repudiated by the Church of the Old Testament.'[31] He suggests therefore that Jesus was rejected as 'Lord' by the Jewish people instead of bringing out clearly that, for a variety of reasons, it was not possible for them either then or later to see in Jesus of Nazareth the exalted *Kyrios*. Nor is the frequently imputed 'fanatical hatred' historically demonstrable; for those Jews who were involved at all in the trial—and it is far from clear who they were—it was a question not of fanaticism, but of a political episode which passed Jesus' contemporaries by, almost without trace. Its worldwide significance became clear only to those who encountered him and believed in him after the resurrection; for all the rest he remained one of the many pseudo-messianic agitators who existed at that time.

How little sympathy and understanding there is of the Jewish
mentality is clear from the way in which the role of the Jews
in the Passion is described by almost all authors. Thus Heinrich
Schlier in *The Relevance of the New Testament* writes: 'The
argument between Jesus and the Jews or the world [note the
typological significance of *the Jews*] which will not give itself
to God, is in general at an end. There has been fulfilled what
was said in the prologue: "He came into his own and his own
received him not" (John 1.11f.).'[32] Normally the whole conflict
of Jesus with Judaism is summed up in this proposition. Jewish
guilt in the trial of Jesus is far greater than that of Pilate, since
'he overlooks what the Jews in their way did not, for of course
they were attempting to kill truth'.[33] When and how did Jesus
ever at that time or now personify 'truth' for the Jews? Pilate
has a lesser responsibility; he wants to rouse compassion for
Jesus among the people: 'With the words "Here is the man!"
he presents Jesus to the Jewish crowd after the scourging ...
He overestimates the effect of a humane appeal to the mob.
It is not moved by the sight of Jesus at all.'[34] If Pilate had
been so touched, why did he have an innocent man scourged
when he had no right to do so and no one demanded it? 'And
now the Jews have recourse to a means which is always effective
when the authority in a state knows it is no longer firmly based
... They drop any show of subordination and threaten the procurator with denunciation to the emperor.'[35] Schlier follows
literally the gospel tradition, although this was meant to provide
something other than a verbatim report of the trial. He continues: 'When he [Pilate] asks, "Shall I crucify your King?"
the spiritual leaders of the nation utter the momentous words,
"We have no king but Caesar" (John 19.15). By that the Jews
through their spiritual leaders abandon their Messianic hope.
They link it to Caesar.'[36] This is a very un-Jewish statement:
for the Jews God was king and they set their hopes on him.
They never linked their messianic hope with the emperor, nor
have they ever abandoned it throughout the centuries.

The author draws the same conclusion from the parable of
the wedding feast in Matthew 22.1–14. Israel, he explains, did
not accept God's offer. 'It is the continual story of the Passion

of God's call among his people.'[37] This parable is not to be related to the action of the Jewish people; it has a deeper meaning and is an exhortation to fidelity addressed to Christians at all times. If it were taken to have merely a contemporary reference, there would be no further message in it for us and it would have ceased to be relevant for Christian proclamation—which it has not. On the contrary, the misunderstanding of God's invitation runs right through the whole history of Christendom.

Eduard Lohse sees the Jews before Pilate in a similar way. They invented the charge of claiming to be king, for they had 'to find some way of convincing the governor that Jesus had to be condemned and executed'.[38] His death did not satisfy them: 'Whereas the Jews only heap mockery and derision on the crucified One, it is a Gentile who realizes that the humiliated One is the Son of God.'[39] Here Lohse takes Mark 15.39 literally; but it is a question here of the theology of the redactor rather than a literal description of what happened at the cross. It would have been impossible for a pagan to describe Jesus here as 'Son of God' in the sense understood by the Church only at a later stage. The idea would never have occurred to any of the disciples before the resurrection, still less to a pagan.

In his article on John's Gospel Josef Blank makes the conflict between Jesus and the Jews particularly sharp, leading to the crucifixion: 'It is important to see that what is portrayed here is evidently not simply a universal "cosmic crisis" in the light of the example of the "Jews": what is predominant here is the crisis of the "Jews", of the Old Testament Jewish religious community ... In the critical conflict between Jesus and the Jews all the religious honorific predicates and privileges in which Jewish self-understanding was rooted are systematically questioned and even directly disputed. It must be observed however that Scripture as such, the Old Testament, as revelation of God to Israel, is not disputed; it is in fact claimed as testimony to Christ. What is disputed is the right of the "Jews" to the Old Testament and the Jewish self-understanding. The controversy drives a wedge so to speak between the Old Testament—which with Moses, Abraham, and the prophets comes to stand at the side of Jesus—and the Jewish self-understanding which is interpreted as unbelief, blindness, obstinacy, and hatred.'[40]

The author is merely repeating here the opinion of the Church Fathers. As early as the first half of the second century Justin Martyr in his Dialogue with Trypho speaks of 'our Sacred Scripture, not yours'. 'This is right and proper, for the Jews are not concerned with God and God's word, but with their own honour.'[41] 'The descent of the "Jews" from Abraham and also their claim to be children of God would be proved if they were to believe. But they do not believe: they want to kill Jesus and therefore can have neither Abraham nor God as their Father.'[42] The sins of Israel against Jesus weighed heavily: 'These are transgressions which touch the covenant relationship itself and which thus render Israel liable to divine penal sanctions.'[43] They are no longer the people of God: 'By rejecting Jesus the "Jews" declare themselves free—at any rate John sees it in this way, especially in the trial of Jesus—from their own foundation and their messianic–eschatological expectation of salvation.'[44] Blank insists that John's Gospel is 'a drastic settlement with the Jewish self-understanding: the Old Testament cult is finally eliminated ... Jesus Christ has taken the place of the ancient religious community of Jerusalem and the temple, the community of the disciples of Jesus takes the place of the "Jews".'[45] This is a view running through the whole of Christian theology: that by 'rejecting Jesus' the Jews themselves are rejected and the Church has taken the place of the Synagogue. Thus from the tenth century onwards in the visual arts the Synagogue has often been depicted at the foot of the cross as thrust out by the triumphant Church and deprived of its sceptre: that is, its former position as the chosen of God.

Romano Guardini sees in the rejection of Jesus by the Jewish people an event of far-reaching historical significance. If it had not been for this 'No', the messianic kingdom could have been set up in the world. As a result of the refusal of the Jews, 'the whole problem of salvation itself was profoundly altered ... The failure of the Jewish people to accept Christ was the second Fall, the import of which can be fully grasped only in connection with the first.'[46] What was the reason for this rejection? The opponents of Jesus desire 'the perpetuance of the old covenant, the victory of the old covenant in the world, of his chosen race'. But they observe that 'the new Rabbi mentions neither the temple nor the Kingdom of Israel; that he questions the world and the value of human existence; so they feel that he is an alien spirit and cannot rest until they have him safely under ground.' Sadducees and Pharisees 'join forces long enough to put to an end the dangerous one'.[47] The people are confused: they have sometimes followed him, but they have also— according to Guardini—tried out of jealousy to kill him (Luke 4.16–30); at the end they stood behind their leaders.

As already mentioned (pp. 50–51, 73), a considerable share of the blame for the death of Jesus is ascribed to the Pharisees. This however does not emerge from the Gospels. On the whole Jesus' teaching was not as fundamentally different from that of the Pharisees as is often claimed. On the chief commandments, love of God and neighbour, there is no opposition (Mark 12.28–34). It is illuminating to compare Matthew 22.34–40 with this. The atmosphere is far less friendly; the scribe does not say that Jesus' answer was 'right', but the lawyer comes 'to test him' (Matt.22.35) and Jesus does not, as in Mark (12.34), say that 'he answered wisely'. In the gospel description a change for the worse has entered in the years between Mark and Matthew, and the later situation of controversy between the early Church and the Jewish community rather than that between Jesus himself and the Pharisees is reflected in Matthew. During the period after A.D. 70 the Pharisees became the creators and leaders of normative Judaism, and the people rallied round them when the temple had been destroyed. But before A.D. 70, as we now know particularly from the discovery of the Qumran writings, there were widespread sects, parties, schisms. If John 9.34 speaks of the excommunication of the man born blind, this cannot be referred at all to the time of Jesus himself when the commandments were interpreted in very different ways by Essenes, Sadducees, Pharisees, Zealots, and probably others, without any group 'excommunicating' another on that account. In the whole course of Jesus' trial there is no mention of the Pharisees apart from the almost impossible detail (John 18.3) that Judas brought a cohort from the high priests and Pharisees to arrest Jesus. In the account of Paul's trial, which is to a certain extent modelled on that of Jesus, the Pharisees take his side against the Sadducees (Acts 23.9), since his teaching is closer than that of the Sadducees to theirs. So much has been written on the trial of Jesus that we shall not enter into greater detail here. There must certainly have been occasional conflicts between Jesus and some of the Pharisees. But it has not been proved, nor can it be proved today, that the latter played a significant part in his trial and condemnation. The authors who take this for granted are *a priori* opponents of the Pharisees (cf. Chapter 3), whose true teaching and conception of the law they know only superficially from manipulated Christian sources and whose true role in the development of Judaism they ignore.

Michael Schmaus is particularly important, since his eight-volume *Katholische Dogmatik* is meant to be an authoritative presentation of Catholic teaching. His opinion on the guilt of the Jews in the death of Jesus is clear and unambiguous: 'With the message of the New Covenant, the Old Covenant becomes obsolete. The Christian revelation on the other hand is eternally young. But, once it is here, those who prepared the way for it have lost any real meaning for their existence. Their tragedy, indeed their guilt, consists in the fact that they do not regard themselves as precursors and consequently are not prepared to be absorbed in the New when the New appears.'[48] Jewish existence, alongside the Church, is paradoxical and can be understood only from an eschatological standpoint: that is, in the light of their conversion at the second coming of Christ.

'The Jews', he continues, 'were bound to be upset by Christ, since he disturbed them in their worldly thoughts and actions ... Their uneasiness ... grew into hatred against him. They decided to eliminate this disturber who frightened them out of their human way of thinking, and they killed him.'[49] The death of Jesus did not need to be violent: 'It became violent as a result of the blindness and obstinacy of the Jews ... When Christ came into his own, his own did not receive him (John 1.11).'[50] They were so rooted in their sin that they did not want to recognize the love of God. Thus Jesus' coming became the hour of the Gentiles: 'Their hour came since the Jews turned away salvation by condemning to death the Redeemer sent by God. From then onwards God's curse lay upon them.'[51] God has still great plans for Israel: 'That part of Israel which continues to resist is to be brought back to its senses through the fall from its former exaltation and through all its afflictions. Only because God cannot forget his people ... he chastises it harshly and often.'[52] This is a congenial explanation of the persecutions of the Jews.

In the third volume he returns to the Jewish problem: 'When however the new age dawned, which had been pre-formed and prepared in the Old Testament, it was not understood or accepted by the representatives of the Old Testament people of God. They rejected Jesus Christ. Consequently they could no longer be partners in God's covenant with men. By rejecting Christ they abandoned their own history, the basis of their own existence as God's people. That is the reason why they themselves are rejected (Rom. 9.31–3; 10.2f.; 11.7–10).'[53] Since then Israel can neither live nor wholly die; it must wait, blinded and hardened. Its place as people of God was occupied by others. From then onwards Israel's political role lies in the fact that 'the whole Old Testament heritage passes over to the Church and above all in the fact that the completion of the Church involves the conversion of the Old Testament people of God'.[54] Anyone who denies the difference between the old and the new people of God is a 'Judaist', a 'Jew' in the sense of John's Gospel, a 'heretic'.[55]

He repeats: 'The early Church's preaching has a different tone when it is addressed to the Jews. By crucifying his envoy the official representatives and leaders of Judaism defied in the most appalling way the God who was offering them salvation. They are invited to appreciate this basic error and to repent.'[56]

Finally, under the heading of *Die Bekehrung des auserwählten Volkes*, Schmaus deals at length with the whole Jewish problem in his fourth volume, *Eschatologie*. Jewish existence remains enigmatic and can be explained only in the light of the Letter to the Romans, as he interprets it: 'Its politicians and theologians misunderstood the promises and handed over to death the one

107

who was to have fulfilled them by the authority of the Father. According to Mark, the last word which Jesus addresses in public to the Jewish people is therefore also a word of judgement (Mark 12.30) [*sic*].'[57] Since the leaders feared that all would believe in him and fall away from them, 'he had to die [John 11.46–53]. But before he could be executed public opinion had to be changed. After many unsuccessful attempts, the leaders managed to rouse the people's passions against him. Thus the whole people came to share in the guilt of its leaders; it became involved in their responsibility. At the decisive moment it deliberately took the blame on itself with all the consequences (Matt. 27.25). In the execution of Christ the whole people set its seal on the rejection of God's envoy. It placed itself under the judgement which hangs above everyone who rejects Christ in unbelief (John 3.18f.) . . . The judgement began with the fall of Jerusalem and continues throughout man's history. Under God's judgement the people cannot live and may not die.'[58] In the Letter to the Romans Paul appears 'like a shipwrecked man who has been saved with a few others in a small boat, while the night is filled with cries of distress from those who are drowning'.[59] But these 'drowning' Jews will also be saved if they are converted to Christ. 'The curse will accompany this people—reduced to a remnant—throughout history and will call down one judgement after another on them, but one day it will come to an end.'[60] For Schmaus this 'curse' and these 'judgements' must mean the persecutions suffered by the Jews also—and particularly—at the hands of Christians. The years 1933 to 1945 are therefore included, since this volume appeared in 1959. It is well known that Schmaus was one of those theologians who adopted a sympathetic attitude towards National Socialism.

Only one sentence need be quoted from Joachim Jeremias' *Jerusalem in the Time of Jesus*, where the guilt of the Jews in the death of Jesus is assumed more or less incidentally: 'It was an act of unparalleled risk which Jesus performed when, from the full power of his consciousness of sovereignty, he openly and fearlessly called these men [the Pharisees] to repentance, and this act brought him to the cross.'[61]

Heinrich Schlier's condemnation is as severe as that of

Schmaus when he speaks of Jesus and the Jews in his chapter on *Das Mysterium Israels*. 'There is an undercurrent of hostility to God running right through the history of Israel in the Old Testament from generation to generation. And it was finally concentrated in deadly hatred against him in whom God—who gives everything—pressed hard on Israel.'[62] What happens now? 'Israel has "fallen" ... it is lying on the ground ... And a "blinding" and "hardening", as promised in Scripture, are fulfilled in Israel, fallen as no other people has fallen.... There is a cover over the rigid Torah and there is a cover over their hard hearts. Hence they no longer even know themselves, they no longer perceive how they are going astray from Israel and becoming pagans (Romans 2), they do not perceive how blindness becomes "hardening" or "obstinacy" on the part of the individual, if they do not submit to Jesus ... the Messiah, their Messiah; they do not perceive in their blindness, as at that time in Jerusalem how with Jesus they constantly deny every Messiah, even the Messiah of their dreams, and play the game of those for whom Caesar is the Messiah.'[63]

It is this blindness which 'fills their history with such great self-consciousness, unrest, resentment, and fanaticism. Yet the people of Israel is punished, not only mentally but also corporeally.'[64] Thus Jerusalem, the City of God, was destroyed: 'The nation was dispersed among all the nations ... sent into the desert. Thus it came about, as the Apostle heard David saying, that "they bend their backs for ever" (Ps. 69.23).'[65] This is a strangely arbitrary exegesis. 'This people ... is no longer a people, nor can it be a "non-people" ... nor yet can it be absorbed in other peoples ... Consequently it lives abandoned in the desert of the world.... The whole torment of that first stay in the desert is constantly repeated in Israel's history, now however without the grace of the continually new revelation and indeed now only kept together by one thing: the curse by which it is burdened and the hatred and aversion of the nations whose godless instincts make a scapegoat for their own sins shamelessly and brutally out of this alien, unprotected people thrown by God into their midst.... We cannot be surprised that this fate of homelessness on the earth and beyond it again gives a sinister appearance to the existence of the Jew, sinister in his hatred of himself and of the nations ... that this homelessness strangely distorts his human shape and strangely confuses his human soul. For the burden of God, the burden of his guilt, the burden of God's wrath, the burden of ineffable suffering, the burden of the world, the burden of man's existence lie upon him.'[66] All this will come to an end only with his conversion to Jesus Christ.

Now what is really surprising is this explanation of the history of Israel in terms of 'the burden of God's wrath'. Who is this terrible, avenging, vindictive God of whom the author speaks? Did he ever really know a Jew or has he simply put together an abstract, theological image of *the* Jew? In the year 1962 had he never heard of the existence of the state of Israel? Did it never occur to him that it is not Israel which is to blame for its history of suffering, but the brutality of the nations—of the *Christian* nations—who put political and religious prejudices and social and financial advantages before Christ's teaching on love of neighbour? 'This therefore is the history of the Jews;' he continues, 'every Jew bears upon him from his fathers the light of God's presence. On every Jew the mark of God's wrath is imprinted. Over every Jew God holds his breath',[67] waiting to see if he will decide for Christ. How can anyone claim to know God's plans so exactly and at the same time ignore so completely historical circumstances? What presumption it is to assume such detailed knowledge of the fate supposedly imposed by God on a people, without consulting this people, its self-understanding, its own conception of history! Here too we have a convenient rationalization, a way of dismissing Christian responsibility for Auschwitz and so many other things by explaining all the sufferings of this people in the light of their supposed guilt in the death of Jesus.

The Jewish people rejected Jesus, since 'the idea of someone who bears the sins of men was bound to seem utterly impossible to the Jews, regarding their relationship to God as exclusively determined by the law'.[68] That is how Eduard Lohse puts it in his *Israel und die Christenheit*: 'When the name of Israel is used by the evangelist [John], it is clearly contrasted with the word "Jew" (John 1.47). The true Israelite is the devout Jew who comes to Jesus and grasps the fact that he is sent by God.... Salvation comes from the Jews (John 4.22). But it is Jesus Christ alone who brings salvation. Where there is faith in him, there is the Israel of God, the chosen people.'[69] Even if the Jews, to whom it was first offered, do not hear it, the word of God still remains valid. The state of Israel has no religious, but only a political significance. Christians read the Old Testament only in the light of Christ, and this means 'that now the Old Testament as distinct from the New really is the old, that the New Covenant has taken the place of the Old.... On the other hand there is no mention in the New Testament of the expectation that the Jews would once more build a state of their own ... it cannot possibly be claimed that the foundation of the state of Israel has anything to do with the fulfilment of Scripture in Jesus Christ.'[70] What Jew would want to claim this? But, after nineteen hundred years of independent history, it is certainly possible to see that the Jewish people, according to its own understanding of Scripture, is called to an independent existence side by side with the Church.

Even with the prophets, Walther Zimmerli writes, it becomes 'ever plainer that Israel will not be able to survive in this event [God's new revelation]. The reality of the people of God can actually survive only in their death before the Holy One who has drawn near, in which everything given to them in the strength of the old promise—land, posterity, monarchy and Temple—are swallowed up together in judgement and the covenant of Yahweh with Israel comes to an end.'[71] Again Israel is denied its right to a continuous, independent existence. 'In his cross, the impossibility (which the prophets had proclaimed) of a righteousness of Israel's own, and the end of the covenant conceived in the law emerges radically ... Here Israel undergoes its deepest humiliation and at the same time the deepest confirmation of its election, in the one rejected by the masses of the historical Israel. Here the old covenant is finished in that the new covenant is established in the midst of Israel in the sacrifice and Resurrection of Christ ... Here every prerogative of Israel according to the flesh is ended, in order that the Israel

111

of God may take shape in the body of the Resurrected One.'[72] To the author it is quite clear 'that in Christ the Old Testament is at an end. . . . Christ is the end of the old covenant and its promise . . . Christ is at the same time the fulfilment of the Old Testament, in which it comes to its ultimate honor.'[73] Zimmerli says nothing about the Israel which continues to live under the 'Old' Testament. Nevertheless, he is one of the very few who regard dialogue with the Synagogue as necessary, since— according to Romans—the Church is still tied to it, even though his use of the expressions 'service of love' and 'witness'[74] are meant to refer mainly to Israel's entry into the Church.

Martin Dibelius' judgement in his *Jesus* is far more severe: 'Jesus' message kept within the frame of Judaism. And yet out of this Judaism grew for him the hostility that brought about his death. On the other hand, in this sentence of death Judaism passed decisive judgment upon itself. For it was not the war with the Romans that left the Jews permanently homeless, but the hostility of the Christians. Such a fateful effect had the opposition between Jesus and the Jews.'[75] By this Dibelius certainly means that the 'hostility of the Christians' was a penalty imposed in the last resort by God on Israel, for seeing in Jesus not the promised Messiah, but the 'arch-heretic'.[76]

Ethelbert Stauffer is one of those who speak most explicitly of the guilt of the Jews for the death of Jesus; he tries to find penal laws in later Jewish writings, often discussing merely hypothetical cases, and then applies them in detail to the trial of Jesus and to his earlier conflicts. 'Precisely with John 5— that is, precisely with the beginning of Jesus' new and decisive effectiveness and this means precisely with the first Torah-conflict—the prosecution of Jesus begins and it finally ends in his condemnation and execution. Jesus was prosecuted as breaker of the Torah and preacher of apostasy. When we know the Jewish laws against heresy, we are overwhelmed by the exact agreement between the penal regulations of the ancient Jewish legal sources and the prosecution of Jesus as it is described for us in the Gospels.'[77]

The condemnation of Jesus occurs in accordance with the laws and 'the destruction of Jesus is the affair of the great

Sanhedrin in Jerusalem'.[78] This is an odd conclusion on the part of a scholar who claims to know the Jewish sources, which belong to a much later date than the trial of Jesus. In order to impose a death-penalty—which scarcely ever happened—the Sanhedrin had to have at least two plenary sessions, and these could not take place at night; the guilt of the accused had to be proved by at least two independent witnesses. It is generally recognized that crucifixion was never a Jewish form of execution. For Stauffer, however, 'Caiphas' conduct of the trial ... was a formally legal masterpiece' in which 'the supreme, spiritual court of all Israel ... unanimously condemned the false prophet, Jesus of Nazareth, to death.'[79] The evangelists are not as well informed as Stauffer: in John there is no trial before the Sanhedrin; in Matthew we find an account of a night session and a very brief mention of a morning session; Mark has a similar description and Luke mentions only a morning session. It is extraordinarily difficult to harmonize the different accounts, particularly since the formulation of the question of the high priest—'Are you the Christ, the Son of the Blessed' (Mark 14.61) or, as in Matthew (26.63) and Luke (22.70), 'Are you the Son of God?'—is not at all Jewish in style. 'Son of the Blessed' and 'Son of God', like 'Lord', *Kyrios*—the translation of the divine name in the Septuagint—was completely strange to Jesus' contemporaries as a messianic concept or title. Man can never be 'Son of God' in the proper but only in an analogous sense. To speak of the conduct of the trial as it emerges only from the Gospels, the description of which was composed only at a later stage, as a 'formally legal masterpiece' is not only inexact, but does not correspond to the facts.

According to Stauffer also, Pilate sincerely strives to release Jesus; but his efforts are in vain, because 'the people, intimidated by the decision of the Sanhedrin and having been for a long time entirely in the hands of the clergy, demanded the release of Barabbas, the scribe [*sic!*] gang-leader, with an overwhelming voice.... After a few decades, Jewry had to pay for this decision with the destruction of Jerusalem.'[80] Anyone who ranks Barabbas among the scribes, without offering the slightest reason for this, can hardly expect the rest of his arguments to be

113

treated with much confidence. The whole episode of Barabbas is disputed and its significance may well be more symbolic than historical.

Even though he is often attacked, however, Stauffer is one of the most widely read New Testament scholars and therefore must be quoted again: 'On the lips of the Jewish accusers the request for the crucifixion may be assumed to have a triple demonstrative significance: crucifixion is for slaves (the pseudo-king is to be mocked by a slave's death), for rebels (Jesus is to die the death of a rebel so that the whole world can see the loyalty of Jewry to the emperor), for false prophets (Jesus is to die the accursed death of the blasphemer to demonstrate before God himself the devotion of his accusers to the Torah).'[81] Against this Pilate's efforts are of no avail, although he struggles 'by every means to secure a just judgement and protection for the innocent one'.[82] 'In the speaking chorus the assembled people pronounce the terrible formula of a conditional self-cursing, "His blood be on us and on our children." This is a divine judgement or—even more—an act of divine worship celebrated by the Roman Procurator in Jerusalem. The representative of the Roman constitutional state solemnly poses ... the question: "Shall I crucify your king?" The supreme spiritual leaders of Jerusalem answer solemnly, "We have no king but Caesar" (John 19.15). It is a great demonstration of loyalty, an imperial liturgy, celebrated by the high priest of the people of God in the centre of the festive city of God.'[83] Fantasy outruns terminology here and carries the author away, struggling to find new and apt expressions—a 'divine judgement', an 'act of divine worship', an 'imperial liturgy'. For anyone familiar with the sober gospel accounts this kind of exaggeration becomes absurd. But how many readers of Stauffer remain uninfluenced by these high-flown expressions? How many are uninfluenced by his emphasis on 'self-cursing' (Matt. 27.25), an expression which—if it was used at all—means not a curse, but the opposite: the masses declare themselves innocent; they take the responsibility on themselves because they are convinced that they have acted rightly. We may leave aside here the question of the historicity of the event; a number of exegetes think that what is involved here is a composition of the redactor which is meant to suggest that the Jewish people of *his own* time on the whole rejected Jesus as Messiah.[84]

Stauffer does not hesitate to combine sentences of Paul and Josephus torn out of their context: 'In the ancient literatures Jews had been described as godless, as enemies of the human race.'[85] Paul appropriates this characterization: 'When the Jew betrays his religious vocation there is nothing but a disagreeable fellow left. Scornfully reversing the Jews' estimate of themselves, Paul turns the ancient reproach into an accusation: they "please not God and are contrary to all men!" For that reason, says Paul, underlining the teaching of Stephen, "the wrath of God is come upon them for ever." Israel is finished (cf. Acts 28.25ff.).'[86]

Stauffer is one of the few authors whose anti-Judaism comes very close to conscious anti-Semitism. This can be seen in his description of Jewish sources on Jesus: 'We perceive here [in the Talmud] the congenial continuation of the Jewish polemic against Jesus which began in Jesus' own time and gained its world-historical victory at the trial of Jesus, in his condemnation, mockery, and crucifixion. It is certainly not easy for a convinced Christian to get to know all the hatred, contempt, dirt, or nonsense which is here poured out on Jesus and Mary.'[87] Understandably, the few talmudic and post-talmudic statements are not flattering, but are those in the Gospels on the Pharisees and scribes and still more the disparaging remarks of the Church Fathers on Judaism any better or fairer? It would not be too much to ask at this point for a clear description of the historical situation which led to these polemics, from which neither side emerges with honour.

Stauffer has not changed his views. It would be interesting to quote in its entirety his article in the triumphalist *Oberammergau Report 70/80*, but two examples may suffice. Among other things he writes there: 'The gospel accounts are fragmentary. The Oberammergau text fills the gaps appropriately, not with poetic fantasy, but here too with biblical material. The list of charges now contains five points: Jesus is a blasphemer of God, a defiler of the Sabbath, an opponent of the Mosaic law, a

preacher of apostasy, a despiser of the tradition of the Fathers.'[88]
He has indeed shown that the Gospels contain very large gaps,
for there is no mention of any of these things in their accounts
of the trial of Jesus. Then the 'taking of evidence' closes and
there follows 'the solemn reading of the three decisive penal
clauses, all of them verbatim from the Old Testament: rebellion
against the legitimate religious authority—death penalty; de-
filing the Sabbath—death penalty; blasphemy—death penalty.
The divine law has spoken. Jesus must die ... I must admit
that I know of no scholarly work of the last hundred years on
the trial of Jesus which could match up to the objective content
of this trial dialogue.'[89]

As we have seen in all the previous chapters, Leonhard
Goppelt takes up a particularly negative attitude towards
Judaism. His judgement on the Jewish attitude to Jesus is therefore not surprising: 'In the Jews' rejection of Him Jesus saw
not only the logical end to His controversy with them, but at
the same time the consistent *conclusion of the conflict between
God and Israel* that had existed ever since the establishment
of their covenant relationship ... Consequently, after His
rejection the Lord of the vineyard would "come and destroy
the tenants, and give the vineyard to others" ... This sentence
... announced ... that what the prophets had threatened was
now taking place in redemptive history, namely, the covenant
people as such were being rejected.'[90] But there is still a chance
for Israel: 'Conversion is the condition for this redemptive
encounter.'[91] 'It is not accidental that this sign of the destruction
of the Temple [the torn curtain in the sanctuary] did not occur
until the year 70 when Israel had herself invalidated the Temple
by a rejection of the gospel which for the time being had all
the marks of finality.'[92] Israel's ignorance, the author maintains,
'is not a tragic mistake, but rather a guilty blindness ... Thus
Israel rejects in guilty disobedience the message of the liberating
righteousness of faith that was proclaimed to them just as it
was to the Gentiles (Rom. 10.14–18).'[93] For Judaism there is
no other way than that of conversion; this is how he sees the
relationship between Church and synagogue: 'Its unbelief is not
a falling away from Christ, but a rejection of Jesus based on

misuse of the revelation of the Law and on blindness concerning Christ's subsequent annulment of the Law ... *Unbelieving Israel is not just a portion of the world.* They are "enemies of God for your sake," "beloved for the sake of their forefathers" (Rom. 11.28). Their enmity is negative service to the Gospel ... Unbelieving Israel [is] ... the opposite counterpart of the ancient people of the covenant, the people which maintains against Christ (Rom. 9.30—10.4; 2 Cor. 3.12–18) the covenant with God abolished by Christ (Rom. 9.4).'[94] As far as the Church is concerned, it must provide 'the service it owes to Israel, namely, unabridged witness to Christ.'[95] This idea is again emphasized in his 'findings' at the end: 'Christianity is the consummation and annulment of Old Testament Judaism and awaits post-Christian Judaism as its opposite, awaits the people of promise striving for its own righteousness and blind to the consummation which has appeared, but still assured of its part in the promises by God's unfathomable grace.'[96] We always find the same theological conviction which is not prepared to read the New Testament in the light of two thousand years of history, in order then possibly to reach the conclusion that more is involved than obstinacy and blindness and that the existence of the Jewish people has its own justification, which does not consist in waiting for the moment of 'conversion'.

Rudolf Bultmann's approach to the Old Testament and to Judaism is too well known for us to go into it in detail here. One quotation may be taken as typical of many which emphasize the culpable Jewish misunderstanding of the message of Christ: 'Thus it happens that at the sight of the actual state of the leaders of the people and of the great mass of the people itself —at the sight of religion frozen into ritualism, at the sight of superficiality and love of self and the world—Jesus' message becomes a cry of woe and repentance.'[97] The charges of 'superficiality' and 'love of the world' are new and surprising and can scarcely be laid against Judaism at that time even by the most prejudiced person. For some people Judaism is gloomily, strictly, slavishly subservient to the law; for others it is light-hearted and frivolous. Are we not bound to see here a prejudice for which all arguments are right as long as they support the thesis that the coming of Jesus and the Church must mean the end of Judaism?

In this connection it is not easy to quote so honourable a Christian martyr under National Socialism as Dietrich Bonhoeffer. But he cannot be left out, since what he says proves once again how deep are the roots struck by anti-Jewish prejudice even in the best of Christian theologians. The following excerpt is from a lecture given in April 1933 and is found in Volume ii of the German edition of his *Gesammelte Schriften*. It was not possible to find anything in the later works which might have contradicted the opinion expressed here. 'The state's measures against Jewry' —April 1 was a day set aside for the boycott of all Jewish businesses—'are connected, however, in a very special way with the Church. In the Church of Christ we have never lost sight of the idea that the "chosen people", which placed the Saviour of the world on the cross, must bear the curse of its action through a long history of suffering. "Jews are the poorest people among all nations on earth, are tormented from time to time, dispersed hither and thither in different countries, have no definite place where they can certainly stay and must always be in fear of being driven out" (Luther, *Tischreden*). But the history of suffering of this people, loved and punished by God, is directed towards the final return of the people of Israel to its God. And this return takes place in the conversion of Israel to Christ. "When the hour comes that this people humbly and penitently turns away from the sin of its fathers, to which it has remained attached to this day with terrible obstinacy, when it begs for the blood of the Crucified to come upon it as reconciliation, then the world will be amazed at the miracle God will work, the miracle he will work on this people ... Then he will gather this people out of all nations and bring it back to Canaan" (S. Menken, 1975). The conversion of Israel: this is to be the end of the people's time of suffering. From this standpoint the Christian Church sees with horror the history of the people of Israel as God's own, free, terrible way with his people. The Church knows that no state in the world can settle with this enigmatic people, since God himself has not yet settled with it. Every new attempt to "solve" the

"Jewish question" breaks down at the significance of this people in salvation history; nevertheless such attempts must constantly be made. The Church's knowledge of the curse which lies on this people prevents it from any cheap moralizing: in fact it is aware also of being humbled as the Church constantly un—faithful to its Lord, when it sees that rejected people and—full of hope—looks to those of the people of Israel who have returned, to those who have come to the one true God in Christ, and it is conscious of being tied to these as brothers.'[98]

Bonhoeffer insists on complete equality of rights for Jewish converts in the Church, on political equality for all Jews and reparation for all the wrongs done to them. Nevertheless he maintains his theological thesis: an example of the influence which Luther still exerts over the centuries even on the best Protestant Christians. If a Bonhoeffer can speak in this way, then we cannot be surprised that the Church generally was a silent onlooker during the years 1933–45; the Jewish people crucified Christ, is accursed and under God's judgement. Certainly men ought not to presume to execute this judgement themselves; but if they do so, are they not *a priori* excusable since in fact they are only concretely carrying out God's will?

The fundamental work of Bousset/Gressmann deals with the religion of Judaism and scarcely touches its position in regard to Jesus. The authors try continually to prove how 'uncreative' and 'imitative' late hellenistic Judaism was.[99] The book ends: 'A new formation had to follow in the gospel before the unity and vitality of genuine and true piety could again emerge from the fermenting chaos. . . . For all this, Judaism had done some honest preliminary work . . . by taking into itself essential ideas of other religions and processing them to a certain extent . . . Judaism was the retort where the different elements were brought together and brewed. Then, through a creative miracle, there followed the new formation of the Gospel.'[100] What is interesting here is not the idea that Judaism prepared the way for the gospel, but that it did so by taking into itself elements of other religions which became important for the gospel. It may be pointed out that Bousset/Gressmann is out of date in this respect and that most exegetes today admit that the New Testament largely emerged precisely from the intellectual background of Judaism. Even Bultmann, who stresses the hellenistic character of primitive Christianity, is out of date on this point.

Adolf Schlatter's interpretation of the history of the Passion is important. He makes it begin, like the Oberammergau Passion Play, with the dismissal of the sellers from the temple. As in the Oberammergau play, he too exonerates Pilate from guilt; the responsibility is made to lie with the whole Jewish people. Thus Jesus brought about 'the decision for or against himself at the market in the temple. He rejected this trading because Israel thus thrust its avarice and acquisitiveness even into the sanctuary and there displayed its greed without shame [the 'market' took place not in the sanctuary, but in the outermost forecourt]. It made his Father's house a house of trade and used the worship of God to produce its own wealth. They valued the temple because of the immense trade it brought them and this he called sin ... He described as corrupt the cult which served to enrich men.[101] Jesus' call to penance 'was a struggle for the law against the community: a community which knows God's will through the law and consequently does not act in ignorance, but commits sin.[102] There is no proof at all for the assumption that Israel valued the temple for the sake of trade. On the day of mourning, still observed on the ninth day of the month of Ab two thousand years later, to commemorate the fall of the first and second temple, there is no mention of finance, but only of penance, atonement, prayer for pardon for such faults as lack of love for the Torah.

For Schlatter the guilt of the Jews for the death of Jesus is quite clear: 'Jesus suffered crucifixion as an act of his people.' It was not a question of the fault of individuals: 'In this decision Israel proved itself to be a united community.... The fact also that he fell into the power of the Gentiles and ended on the cross was felt as particularly hard, because Israel had thus expelled him from its ranks. Consequently the blame for his death is not laid on Pilate, and Israel cannot be excused on the ground that it was through the injustice of the Roman authorities that Christ was crucified.'[103] This may serve as a summary expression of the general opinion of German theo-

120

logical teaching of the past fifty years; in one form or another the attitude is always the same, and it has not changed even in recent years after the many discussions on 'deicide' at the Second Vatican Council.

We may close with some examples from French works. Marie-Joseph Lagrange in his *Le Messianisme chez les juifs* is consistently anti-Judaistic and assumes the guilt of the Jews in the trial and death of Jesus as an established fact, since they did not want a suffering Messiah. In this work however he is concerned exclusively with the wrong ideas of the Jews about the Messiah and ends his comments: 'Among so many people devoted to a Messianism less fantastic but nevertheless more material than that of their ancestors, Judaism even today has many who are attached to another ideal, who are plunged in sorrow and anxious about their salvation. They are not even tempted to dream of a warrior-Messiah, for which their people, their seers, and their teachers had all longed. May they come to recognize the true Messiah in the crucified Jesus.'[104]

Joseph Bonsirven's *On the Ruins of the Temple* deals with the history of the Jewish people after the time of Jesus, but the author sees no difference in their attitude before or after: 'It is certain that the general feeling of the majority of Jews, in the first centuries, in regard to the Founder of Christianity, was one of venomous hatred.'[105] He quotes examples from the Talmud and the much later *Toldoth Yeshu*. In another place he speaks of the rejection of Jesus and its consequences for Judaism. The envoy of God 'has come, producing striking proof of his mission, the witness of Moses and the Prophets ... His own received him not; his message did not correspond to their ambitions ... Then Judaism, having rejected the only one who could broaden and transfigure it, was condemned to be shut up more and more narrowly in its fundamental antinomy and stifling exclusiveness.'[106]

The *Introduction to the New Testament* by A. Robert and A. Feuillet, much used by Catholic theologians, mentions the role of the Jews in the Passion here and there, merely incidentally, and it is generally very cautious in its statements. Nevertheless, we find sentences like this: 'Him whom the

121

Jews had nailed to the cross, God has raised up',[107] as if the fact were not open to discussion.

Similar passages are found in Xavier Léon-Dufour's *Dictionary of Biblical Theology*, which is also widely consulted. In the article on 'Judgment' we read among other things: 'Still there is one crime which, more than all the rest, calls down the divine judgment. This crime, in which human unbelief reached the summit of its malice in a sham display of legal judgment, is Jesus' trial and condemnation to death.' It is true that the author speaks immediately of the divine judgement which will fall on all sinners, but he adds that this 'will affect first of all "those who are in Judea", the leaders in guilt'.[108] Under the heading of 'Persecution' we read that Jesus, like the prophets, was persecuted and oppressed by those to whom he had been sent. 'In condemning Him, the leaders of Israel heaped high the measure of the crimes of their fathers.'[109] But the wrath of God will come upon the persecutors, particularly those who became hardened and also persecuted Jesus' disciples.

On the whole however these last two works are reserved and mention only cautiously the part of the Jews in the Passion, concentrating immediately on the universal theological significance of Jesus' death. It is different with Pierre Benoit. His three volumes, *Exégèse et Théologie*, the last of which appeared in 1968, clearly and expressly attribute to *the* Jews the blame for the death of Jesus and make them responsible for their fate since then.

In his review of Jules Isaac's *Jésus et Israel*, he writes that it would have been impossible for the Jewish masses not to recognize Jesus as the special envoy of God, but they wanted to follow only a victorious Messiah. 'Abandoned by the mob, rejected by the leaders, Jesus was indeed repulsed by his own people, even if—or, rather, because—this people did not want to renounce itself in order to believe in him.'[110] The Gospel accounts give a correct picture of the historical Pilate: 'It does in fact emerge from the four Gospels that, if the Romans ratified and carried out the sentence of death on Jesus, the sentence itself really came from the side of the

Jews ... By the voice of its leaders Judaism as religion rejected him who offered himself to lead it in God's name to the
culmination of its religious vocation.'[111] We can no more make
each and every Jew responsible for the death of Jesus than we
can make the individual responsible for the sin of Adam.
Nevertheless, 'in both cases we can speak of collective responsibility in virtue of the solidarity of nature or race'.[112]
As everyone is born burdened by original sin, we might say,
'by analogy, that every member of the Jewish race bears the
penalty of the crime of Calvary in that he receives from his
race a religion deprived of that messianic flowering which its
God offered to it and which the responsible leaders of this
religion did not want at the decisive moment. In both instances
of these collective sins the heir is born ruined. It is of course
not his fault, but that of his ancestors. Nevertheless ruin is
imposed on him, with all its consequences.'[113] It is not this
alone, he continues, which is the cause of anti-Semitism.
'Another, not less important reason lies in Israel's failure in
its mission, making it restless, a burden to itself and a burden
to others.' As long as Israel does not recognize Jesus as
Messiah, 'it will make itself unhappy and will make the
world unhappy, provoking the antipathy and the persecutions
of which it then complains so bitterly'.[114] In a footnote he
adds that the Jews began the persecution of Christians when
they persecuted Paul, and this to a certain extent explains the
historical events. The Jews therefore are to blame for their
own suffering. Certainly, Benoit thinks that the brutal persecutions and some of the excuses for these are deplorable, but
he also thinks that Jules Isaac goes too far in trying to rouse
compassion by his comments. It is true that Jesus himself
says: 'Father, forgive them, for they know not what they do.'
Benoit relates these words exclusively to the Jews and concludes: 'This very prayer assumes quite rightly that their
fathers have "done" something evil and that they need "forgiveness". For them this forgiveness will consist in the re-
discovery by the mercy of the Father of this grace of the true
Messiah which they refused when it was offered to them.'[115]

The author maintains his opinion in a later article, reprinted from a lecture which he gave after the Vatican declaration on Judaism: 'In any case, he [Jesus] clearly foresaw the refusal of his message by the religious leaders of Israel and their followers, a culpable refusal, because they had shut themselves off from the light. They are those whom the fourth Gospel designates as "the Jews" . . . in an abridged account which must be rightly understood: not all the children of the chosen people, since there were some who "received" Jesus; but those who "did not receive" him. And he announced the punishment: the loss and destruction of the temple; that is, the transformation of the old economy of salvation. The refusal of official Judaism was completed by the crucifixion of Jesus. It emerges from the Gospel accounts of the Passion that this was definitively the work of the Sanhedrin . . . the Roman authority had to collaborate because it had withdrawn from the Jews the right to put anyone to death. But it did so by yielding to the pressure of the leading Jews who were principally responsible.'[116] He argues in the light of the thesis—which is not proved and in the present state of research cannot by proved —that the right to carry out the death penalty had been taken away from the Jewish authorities. He continues: 'Such a decision by the supreme authority in Israel, rejecting Jesus and his message, cannot be reduced to the limits of a deplorable but momentary misunderstanding, due to the cowardice of some "Jewish" collaborators. It commits the people by the voice of its authorized leaders.'[117]

Benoit admits that no one can penetrate into the deepest thoughts of another person and decide the extent of his responsibility. Nevertheless, for him it is a certainty of faith that 'official Israel evaded its mission at the decisive moment and rejected its Messiah. Whatever allowances are to be made, this historical fact with its theological implications cannot be denied.' Admittedly he says then that the mob which had been roused before the praetorium could not represent the Jewish people and that the cry, 'his blood be upon us and on our children', may be more a theological than an historical utterance; but it is true, for it 'expresses in advance the resolute and obstinate resistance which the mass of Israel will oppose

124

to the propagation of the gospel'.[118] He returns again to the same point: 'It might be said that the Jewish people was scarcely present before the praetorium in Jerusalem, but it must be recognized that afterwards, by its behaviour in the whole Graeco-Roman world, it amply ratified the decision of Good Friday.'[119]

Later he repeats this assertion several times. For example: 'The religious authority of the Jewish people assumed the real responsibility for the crucifixion. Israel closed itself up against the light ... This resistance to God's plan was maintained throughout the centuries, up to our own time.'[120] He then invites every Christian to pray for the Jews, that God may pardon them, and says that Christians too should deplore the wrongs they have done to Jews in the course of history. But 'on the plane of salvation-history the Jewish people as such committed a special fault.... This fault may be compared in a way with original sin: without involving the responsibility of each descendant, it makes him inherit the ancestral bankruptcy. Every Jew suffers from the ruin undergone by his people when it refused [Christ] at the decisive moment of its history.'[121]

This is the second time that the comparison with original sin occurs. In another article he returns to it a third time. Apparently even he does not find it easy to load the collective guilt for the death of Jesus on so many Jews who are in good faith. That is why he looks again for a solution in the comparison with original sin: 'The sons of a dishonest banker ... are innocent of the malpractices of their father; nevertheless, they are ruined at birth. Likewise, in an analogical sense, we may say that the Jews today are not themselves guilty of the refusal presented by their ancestors at the decisive turning point of their mission, but they inherit this lapse which has compromised their universal mission. They receive from their fathers a religious system which is no longer completely in accordance with God's plan.'[122] The Church is the true Israel; Judaism has lost this honorific title because it rejected Christ. But for Judaism the Church has only love and hope, hope for its final conversion. Certainly the Church must continuously remind this rebel people of the harsh truth of its sin, without however lapsing into anti-Semitism. It prays for them—and this is how Benoit ends his reflections—that the day may soon come when Israel will understand what wealth and fulfilment entry into the Church would mean for it.

It might be thought that too much space has been given here to Benoit's ideas. But he is one of the best-known modern Catholic New Testament scholars. He is also one of the most influential professors of the Ecole Biblique in Jerusalem, where selected priests are sent for post-graduate studies in Scripture. He is also editor of one of the best international biblical reviews, the *Revue Biblique*. That is why his observations, so boldly and clearly stated, have a special importance. There are some few theologians, specialists in Jewish-Christian relationships, who adopt a view different from that of Benoit. Otherwise however his theory of the guilt of the Jews for the death of Christ and the consequences of this guilt is fully shared by many others, even if they do not express their views with the same imperturbable frankness and force as he does.

6

'From Generation to Generation'

The influence on Students of theology today of
the teaching on Judaism in theological literature

A few years ago, after a special course on 'Introduction to the
New Testament' in the theology department of a German
university, the students, working independently during the
vacation, produced a number of essays. These, almost without
exception, were well constructed, displayed diligence and effort,
and proved—especially in the notes—that the students had
attentively consulted the relevant works on the subject. The
present author—who gave the lectures—was at pains to give
an objective description of Judaism between the Old and
New Testaments: that is, not as 'late Judaism', but as a living,
evolving religion and culture. Far from succumbing to ossifica-
tion and corruption, Judaism was flourishing and produced a
variety of new trends. Even though the different groups fought
one another—as, for example, the Sadducees and the Qumran
sect—the time was still rich in promising ideas which permitted Judaism to survive after the year A.D. 70 and maintain
an independent existence for two thousand years under the
most difficult conditions. The lectures aimed at explaining the
rabbinic interpretation of Scripture, the love of God and his
word; in brief, to penetrate to the real spirit of Judaism.
The continuity also between the pre- and post-Exilic stock of
ideas, the greater depth and devotion of religious practice were
stressed and all this illustrated with the aid of such works as
Pirke Aboth ('Sayings of the Fathers'). It seemed particularly
important to explain the biblical-Jewish ideas of the Messiah

from a non-Christian standpoint and in the light of this to show that a personality with the claims of Jesus of Nazareth, as these are presented in the Gospels, would in normal circumstances be unacceptable to a devout Jew and that this need not involve any sin or guilt on the part of the latter.

It was therefore with a feeling of optimism that I set the students as an essay theme: 'How do you explain the general lack of understanding for Jesus on the part of his contemporaries?' In this respect, the students, after following the lectures, might have been expected to attempt to explain that it was almost impossible for a God-fearing Jew, faithful to the Torah, in virtue of his legitimate understanding of Scripture, to see in Jesus the promised envoy of God with whom the new age was to have dawned. The point had been made in the lectures that it was a question here of completely different messianic concepts: the Jewish ideas were based on a very ancient tradition and were to some extent coloured by the situation at the time; they were not obviously applicable to Jesus' messianic claims. The students might have been expected to allow for the mental climate of the age in their attempts at an explanation and thus to get rid of the ideas of 'self-inculpated stubborness', 'culpable blindness', 'malicious rejection of the Son of God'. It was assumed that a student in 1970 would be in a position also to think in terms of form- and redaction-criticism and thus to distinguish between Jesus' own time and the time of the definitive composition of the New Testament writings. But, on the contrary, the Gospels were understood in a fundamentalist way, as verbatim reports of events in the time of Jesus. This attitude may have changed in the course of their later exegetical studies; it seems doubtful however whether this will drastically change their view of Judaism and its attitude to Jesus and his role in the world. Their opinions, probably already settled by school and home background—the liturgy also plays a role in this respect— were most probably too firmly rooted and were merely confirmed by the books they had studied.

The students made use indiscriminately of Catholic and Protestant authors for their work. Their opinions—and this is the crucial point—they drew without exception from the books examined in the previous chapters of the present work; the lectures had practically no influence on them. It should be stressed once again that neither in the department of theology as a whole nor among the students in particular was there a sign of any inclination to anti-Semitism. The anti-Judaism which could not but be noticed in all the essays arose wholly and entirely from the works of reference which were read and extensively quoted by the students. Vatican II had exercised no influence here; on the whole the students had scarcely read the Declaration on Judaism, nor—despite all the efforts of the lecturer—had they understood its background. The reasons for this state of affairs are probably complex, but the main reason seems to be that the printed work, the undisputed authority of its author—usually famous—exercised a far deeper and more lasting influence than a course of lectures on a particular occasion.

In what follows the essays will be left to speak for themselves. They are not arranged in a thematic order, but quoted simply as they come. Although their anti-Judaistic attitude made no difference to the marking, the students were greatly surprised by the objections raised on this account and regarded the criticism as unfair and unintelligible. For reasons which will easily be understood, no names are given here either of the university itself or of the students who took part. The essays are quoted as a typical example of how much modern students of theology, even after the utmost exertion of an objectively informed teacher, are influenced by the relevant literature. Experience shows that only those who later take up a special course of study in a department of Jewish studies eventually change their view, while the average pastor or teacher remains under the influence of the literature he has conscientiously studied. Examples of this can be found in sermons, especially in Holy Week, and in the general agreement —which still persists—with plays like that of Oberammergau.

We may refer here to a book which appeared recently, *Judentum im christlichen Religionsunterricht*, which throws a critical light on Protestant religious instruction in schools.

There we read: 'In order to be able to judge fairly and comprehensively the questionable treatment of Judiasm in Protestant religious instruction in Germany today, we must extend the horizon of our analysis. The reason is that the basis for directives, teaching schemes, and schoolbooks is provided by the presentations of Judaism and its relationship to Christianity in the *publications* of Protestant New Testament scholars. . . . And how teachers and pastors deal in religious instruction with Judaism and its relationship to Christianity depends . . . on whether and how they were informed about these things in the course of their studies.'[1]

In his introduction the author speaks of the necessity of an investigation of 'anti-Judaism in the publications of German New Testament scholars since 1945'. How right he was is clear from the following essays.[2]

One student begins with the question whether 'Israel's hardening' in regard to Jesus was really so great and why exactly Jesus was not accepted as the Messiah 'for whom the people had been waiting with longing for thousands of years'. On the last page he gives the answer: 'For thousands of years the Jewish people were prepared, instructed, persuaded, and provided with prophecies, in order one day to receive the Messiah. He came to them. But the people believed in their scribes, their theologians, their priests . . . They had attended carefully in their religious instruction. For they were God's chosen people, experts in religion, experts in everything that concerned God. Christ demanded a total conversion and they were not ready for this. It is only fair to point out that this student added that we today are also not ready for it.

In the course of his essay, when he speaks of the Jews, he uses the expression *Judenvolk* ('nation of Jews') which in German has overtones of anti-Semitism. On the disputes with the Pharisees and others he follows the Gospels closely. The 'theologians and scribes at that time . . . did not accept him, they accused him, wanted to bring him down and finally had him crucified by the governor, Pontius Pilate'. He quotes in particular Matthew's Gospel with its 'Woes' (Chapter 23) and takes literally everthing that is said there. On Jewish messianic ideas he quotes a book unknown to me, P. J. Cools, O.P., *Die biblische Welt*, vol. ii (1965): 'For most if not all Jews at the time of Jesus, the idea prevailed of an earthly, national, and political kingdom which would give them power to rule over the nations.' They did not or would not understand that Isaiah 53 refers to the Messiah, 'for most Jews dreamed of a glorious and triumphant king and refused to recognize a despised and suffering Messiah (Matt. 16.21–3)'. The explanation of the Jewish exegesis of this chapter, as given in the lectures, passed over the heads of the students without leaving a trace.

As far as the Pharisees 'are concerned, in their almost weird way of observing the law, they numbered the steps they could take on the Sabbath and discussed the egg laid by a hen (versed in the law) on the Sabbath'. This is quoted from A. Voegtle, a well-known New Testament scholar, in his *Entführung in das Neue Testament* which appeared in German in 1962–4. Out of all the explanations they had received of the spirit and achievements of the Pharisees what stuck most firmly in their memories was the egg laid on the Sabbath. Hence 'the necessary consequence of this all-too-Jewish conception of religion' was 'that many were satisfied with the literal fulfilment of the law. A reward was expected for keeping the law and likewise a punishment for not keeping the rules.' External observance was everything; 'the motives of action frequently receded into the background. As a result the true meaning of religion was bound to suffer.' The Pharisees as 'set apart' 'claimed the first places, the highest positions, places of honour at banquets and first seats in the synagogues'. They despised and cursed all others (John 7.49). Again the Gospel account is taken literally.

In the 'late Jewish' understanding of the idea of election the emphasis was 'less on responsibility to others than on one's own righteousness, self-assertion, and election, which practically lived on the rejection of others' (quoted from Voegtle). Jesus turned to those who did not know the law and brought them a new message of salvation. 'His criticism of casuistry and legalism brought him into conflict with the

Pharisees. His free attitude to the Sabbath, purity regulations, and the precept of cultic taxes meant in the last resort taking seriously the precept of love as God's supreme demand. The Pharisees could not regard all this as anything but unpardonable lawbreaking.' Jesus acted with 'ultimate divine authority.... This claim the Pharisees and scribes could regard only as presumption and blasphemy and consequently demanded his death.' Martin Metzger's *Grundriss der Geschichte Israels* (1967) is given as the source. Judaism, faithful to the law, is here judged even more negatively than by Metzger himself, and the Pharisees are made responsible for the death of Jesus.

There are some interesting observations by an older Japanese student, who must have taken his opinions from European authors. He writes on the Letter to the Romans and mentions more or less incidentally: 'Although the Gentiles have been engrafted on to the tree of redemption, God will cut them down more rigorously than the Israelites who were corrupted.' These 'Israelites relied mainly on their own actions in keeping the law and not on faith, and could not be justified'. 'In late Judaism this concept [righteousness] became forensic.' In Romans 'the Jewish doctrine of salvation is disputed: this was based on legalistic piety and consciousness of election, circumcision'. It is not clear what he means by a 'doctrine of salvation based on circumcision'. As source he gives a biblical lexicon published in 1968. This is a good example of the way in which an Asiatic Christian, belonging to a quite different tradition, has assimilated and reproduced western prejudices almost unconsciously.

In an essay on the same theme one student comes at once in his list of contents to the 'Fate of the *ancient* chosen people of the Jews'. It is not surprising that he speaks later of circumcision as if it were the essential item of the Jewish faith. In his explanation of Romans 9–11 we find: 'God did not withdraw salvation from Jewry without their fault. The rigid, constrained view of the law did not permit any understanding for the message of Christ. They were no longer open enough to faith in Christ. But God spoke clearly and unequivocally to the Jews through Christ, and he still speaks to them through specially authorized representatives. It is therefore human misunderstanding of God's intentions and thus culpable.' This essay has neither notes nor bibliography, but it is clear that the statements are directly based on the works of the authors quoted in earlier chapters.

The next essay is the best from the standpoint of structure, style, and evaluation of the very varied literature. Consequently it deserved the mark 'very good'. This student was older than the others and had already completed a course in history. We must therefore observe all the more sadly that his work too is full of the old prejudices. In the very first sentence he speaks of the 'rejection of Jesus of Nazareth by the Jews of his time' and calls this 'tragic'. According to him the Jews after the Babylonian exile were not a nation, but Judaism was 'established as an autonomous temple-polity'. He appeals very frequently to the work of Schürer without ever mentioning how out of date and how lacking in scholarly exactitude it is. So, for example, Israel's faith suffered 'a contraction and fossilization'; 'what was lacking to the Jewish faith was the immediate present' (quoted from Bornkamm's *Jesus of Nazareth*). The 'arguments with the Pharisees mounting up to open hostility' in the Gospels are understood as eye-witness reports, although, according to Klausner, Jesus was very close to the Pharisees. The exegesis of the scribes he calls 'casuistry'; occasionally—he says—they reach 'conclusions in regard to moral life which (as a result of their legalism) amount to a slap in the face for the essence of morality'. The following pages largely consist of one quotation from Schürer after another: for example, the result of fulfilling the law was 'an incredible externalization of the religious and moral life'. The moral task 'breaks down into an endless atomistic mass of individual tasks and duties the fulfilment of which threatened to become and actually did become a petty and perverse zeal'. 'Jesus' cures are linked on every occasion with an invitation to the bystanders to decide between morality and the letter of the law.' The examples given are of cures on the Sabbath. It is not clear why he opposes the concept of 'morality' to that of the 'letter of the law'.

'Against pharisaic casuistry' Jesus wants to bring out the fact that the 'Sabbath exists for man. For the Pharisees, meaning to inculcate respect for the Sabbath precept, make it a burden for men.' Here too he invokes Schürer. He takes literally the reference to *qorban*: the rabbis of Jesus' time declared such a vow binding; later it was different. How does he claim to know so exactly the treatment of this kind of vow in the first century? All the sources which mention oaths are of a later date. In order to stress Jesus' new righteousness, he says: 'The idea of reward, literal fulfilment of the law, casuistry, and the thought of recompense are overcome. The Pharisees regarded this as abolishing law and tradition.'

Jewish messianic ideas were 'worldly, political, and national' —here he makes use of both Förster and Schürer. The Pharisees did not examine Jesus' miracles closely enough; 'they did not weigh and balance with sufficient care the phenomenon of Jesus as a whole, but, sure of their knowledge of Scripture and their righteousness, demanded his rejection and put this into effect when the opportunity arose by the sentence of death.' Since in fact the Pharisees 'were unable to recognize Christ's claim they resolved to catch and execute him as a heretic.'

On the most diverse occasions this writer returns to the piety of the Pharisees and mentions particularly their extra-ordinarily improbable 'exploitation of widows', adding how-ever, as if by way of excuse, that this 'was probably the result of their own poverty'. This he took from Leipoldt/ Grundmann. In every case we find with the Pharisees an 'externalization and materialization of ethics'. His knowledge of the position of women he draws from the same work: 'The whole trend of Jewish thinking after Old Testament times displays a constant belittling and lowering of respect for women, even by comparison with their position in ancient Israel.' An improvement in their position came about through Jesus, as is proved by the group of women who followed him. This student knew very little of Paul's statements on the same theme, nor had he gone into the question of the subordinate position of women in the Church throughout the centuries. His second section, 'Jesus and the Pharisees', he sums up in this way; 'It is mainly their fault' that Jesus was not acknowledged as Messiah. 'They made the law and knowledge of the law into absolutes and declared Jesus a heretic.' Their momentary success however turned into a historical defeat.

The next piece of work is less intelligently set out, but is closer to the average in quality. Its author came from a village, and the essay reveals a conservative mentality and a naive piety. The very first sentence sets the tone: 'For a student of theology it is interesting to investigate how exactly it came about that Jesus was not understood as Messiah by the Jews, and even nailed to the cross.' When he writes of the 'moral and religious state of the people of Israel' in the time of Jesus, he produces these clichés on the Pharisees: They 'were of a Jewish-religious-national strictness. Holiness based on works, arrogance, and hypocrisy were part of the ordinary routine with them. Their view of religion was very superficial. . . . Under the influence of the Pharisees the Jewish people were inclined to a religiosity without genuine piety. Moral life was in decay.'

His section on 'Israel and the Messiah' borders on the fantastic. He tries to perceive in the most diverse passages of the Bible an exact prediction of Jesus' coming and a description of his person. 'The Messiah is Son of God (Ps.2.7) and Son of man. . . . The virgin birth (Isa.7.14) and place of birth (Mic.5.1) are foretold', as also the time of his coming! 'Passion and suffering are announced (Ps.22; Zech.12.10; Isa. 53). He rises again from the dead (Ps.16.10; Hos.13.14) . . . Through these prophecies the Messiah was precisely delineated and recognizable.' This last piece of wisdom he found in J. Ibach, *Die Geschichte der Kirche Christi* (1917), a little known book which I have not seen, the content of which however can be imagined. The student concerned had remained unaffected by modern Old Testament exegesis. It is natural to find in this context 'the very superficial view of religion and the formal legalistic piety' of the Pharisees, who were hoping for 'the establishment of an international kingship with world-dominion'. The works quoted are mostly obsolete and by unknown, long outdated authors. For him even 'the picture of the Messiah drawn by the prophets is completely distorted: it had become an illusion of earthly power, a picture without any mental or moral sublimity, it was the picture of a carnally and nationally conceived Messiah.' The fact that the people were changed for the worse must be ascribed mainly to the Pharisees. 'The fact that the people did not accept Christ is described by Roman Guardini as a second Fall.' They did not recognize Jesus as Messiah, for 'there was too much hypocrisy among the people. Outwardly conscientiousness and fidelity to the law, but inwardly hardness of heart and sin without knowledge or penance.' His source is Matthew's Gospel. 'The Pharisees' hard-heartedness was so great that they perverted the God-given law in such a way that it involved the death of God's Son.' He refers once more to Guardini: the people had become marionettes in the hands of the Pharisees. He mentions 'the second Fall' of the Jewish people several times in the course of his essay.

The end of his work has some significance. Despite all liturgical renewal and the now completely changed prayer for the Jews on Good Friday, this student quoted the altar missal which he had probably examined in his village church and in which—despite Vatican II—nothing had been changed. Before quoting the prayer in full, he provides a personal introduction: 'The task remains for us Christians to proclaim Christ to the other brothers and sisters and to pray for them. Naturally, it remains for us a source of distress that the Jews, the chosen people of God, have not up to the present time recognized the Messiah. At this point human resources fail and we must place the fate of the Jews in the hands of God. It is therefore only proper to join in the Church's prayer.' There follows the old Good Friday prayer for the 'perfidious Jews', on whose hearts a veil lies and who are blinded: may they soon be 'rescued from their darkness'.

Can this be dismissed as the unscholarly work of a very mediocre student? It is not as easy as that. Its author had read a lot of the relevant literature belonging to the period 1917–69. He also had forty-eight footnotes. The striking thing is that he consulted a whole range of third- and fourth-class works whose authors are forgotten today and which are scarcely to be found in libraries. One got the impression that he had brought with him from school and perhaps also from home a strong anti-Jewish bias and that his reading had only strengthened this. His inadequate work cannot be regarded as typical, but it does display a kind of piety which can certainly still be found among many simple churchgoers. If this student becomes a priest, his opinions—with all the prejudices expressed here —will certainly be passed on in sermons and instruction. It must be added that it was impossible to enter into a frank discussion with this taciturn and apparently embittered student. The present author got the impression that she was dealing here with the kind of 'authoritarian personality' described so finely by Theodor W. Adorno in his book with the same title and that the man's depreciative attitude to people of different opinions was not restricted to Jews. Even he could not be described as anti-Semitic; but if he were ever to encounter a political-social anti-Semitism, he would certainly welcome it with some sympathy.

The next essay begins with the sentence: 'As a result of the obstinacy of the Jews and particularly of the Pharisees Jesus had to suffer death.' The student then admits that he wants to study the Gospels and the history of that time in order to establish the accuracy of this assertion. His opinion is that the scribes 'interpreted the Bible very casuistically and for this they were very strongly reprimanded by Jesus when he spoke of their meanness and insincere behaviour and described them as hypocrites'. Here too we find an uncritical, unhistorical view of the Gospels. Like the other students and like the few authors whom he quotes, he criticizes the distorted image of the Messiah in Judaism, which was only waiting for a national-political liberation. He too speaks of the decadence of 'Judaism' as compared with the earlier Israelitic religion. 'Rabbinic Judaism saw the law merely as an enormous number of individual rules and made their observance the embodiment of religion.' At every turn he follows closely the statements and accounts of the Gospels and applies the methods neither of form- nor of redaction-criticism. It was the Pharisees' fault

137

that 'the fulfilment of the law became a burden'; as evidence he quotes Matthew 23.4: 'They bind heavy burdens, hard to bear, and lay them on men's shoulders; but they themselves will not move them with their finger.' He too speaks of the 'danger of externalization' in the 'legalistic piety of the Pharisees and scribes': hence the 'woes' of Jesus on both groups in Matthew 23. Since Jesus did not bring about 'political liberation and increased prosperity', his messianic claims had to be rejected. Jesus' attitude was bound to be a scandal to the teachers of the law 'who observed the purity regulations only in order to be so much more justified in God's sight'. He ends his brief essay very abruptly: 'The reasons given show the great gulf that existed between Judaism and Jesus. But they also show that the picture of the Pharisees and the other parties in the gospel is not objective.' This sentence he has taken from the lectures; but the trend of his essay is in the opposite direction, the Gospels being continually quoted in order to show that the Pharisees, legalistic piety, Jewish messianic expectations are correctly described there. He did not find any way out of the dilemma between his own traditional view and the presentation given in the lectures.

More than one essay takes as its motto John 1.11: 'He came to his own and his own received him not.' The writer of the following essay found it odd that the Messiah was expected by the Jewish people, that Jesus claimed to be the Messiah, and yet that he had to end his life miserably on the cross. He speaks, incidentally, not of the Jewish people, but of the 'Israelitic religious community'. His favourite authors are Schmaus, Braun, and Daniel-Rops. He follows these 'sources' faithfully and has scarcely any ideas of his own. Thus he copies Herbert Braun word for word: 'The Pharisees aimed at "bringing the whole of life into the co-ordination system of the commandments".' Jesus on the other hand regarded obedience to the Torah as dangerous for man. The only new point to be found in this student's work was his criticism of the Jews for not being willing to learn from children. Jesus set up the children as teachers 'because of their ability to accept a gift without ulterior motives, without calculation or guile'—this was 'quite un-Jewish'. Jesus had to die because the Jewish masses did not recognize him and were easily persuaded by 'the ruling class'. The opinion that the people had become a toy in the hands of the Pharisees and scribes occurred constantly in all the essays, as indeed it is found also—as we have seen—in the work of many scholars.

The next essay also begins with John 1.11: 'He came to his own and his own received him not.' In his introduction this student then continues: 'Israel, his people, does not offer him [the Messiah] any faith, it does not recognize him as such; the people of God does not understand him, and he ends finally as one criminal among others on the cross.' He quotes Daniel-Rops when speaking of Israel's election: 'A national pride filled the soul even of the most wretched Jew when he remembered that he belonged to the chosen people.' For this people, with a wrong idea of the transcendent God and of his proper historical role, the incarnation was incomprehensible. Such a 'humiliation' of God was inconceivable. And therefore a man who claimed to be the Son of God and even to be of the same nature as God, the incarnate God, the God-man—such a man had to be condemned as blasphemer. John 10.33ff. is quoted as proof of this. As with the others and also with a number of the authors already quoted, the statements attributed by the evangelists to Jesus are understood as the *ipsissima verba* of Jesus and the conclusions based on this questionable evidence. The Jews could not summon up faith in an invisible kingdom of God, they needed 'signs and wonders'. 'They had become so fixed in the expectation of the objectively perceptible dawn of the kingdom of God that they could not recognize Jesus as the Messiah.'

As usual, the essay had a section on 'Jesus and the Law'. The writer sometimes quotes, sometimes judges for himself: ' "In Judaism a casuistic system had developed out of the effort to fulfil as exactly and comprehensively as possible the Torah, the commandment of God, which with its network of ethical, juridical, and cultic rules embraced the whole existence of the religious individual" (quoted from Josef Blank). But Jesus rebelled against casuistry, rubricism, Pharisaism.' For Jesus the

139

law existed for man and 'not *vice-versa*, man for the law'. He rejects 'the casuistic-rubricistic mode of fulfilling the law', for this blocks the way to 'man's becoming human'. He sums up, quoting Daniel-Rops: 'Jesus' proclamation "is a rejection of the public teaching" . . . And the consistent carrying out of his proclamation . . . finally brought him to death on the cross.'

The student reaches the conclusion: so Jesus had to be 'a blasphemer, since he had claimed divine sonship, even consubstantiality with God'. Here a much later, highly developed Christology is indiscriminately mingled with original Gospel sources, events in Jesus' time with statements of the redactors of the New Testament writings. Even the language in another paragraph would be ridiculous if it did not display an ignorance which must be taken seriously: 'Jesus clashed totally with his people by turning against petty casuistry, against rubricism, legalism, formalism, rigorism, and not least Pharisaism in the interpretation of the law. The inevitable result was the rejection of Jesus by Israel.' It is only right to add that this piece of work contains some things which are correct (for example, on the unbelief of the disciples before the resurrection). But a detailed analysis would reveal a failure to understand, a lack of sympathy and of insight into the reality of Jewish thought, almost everywhere. Almost all the works quoted here represent scholarship at a popular level by second-rate authors.

There is nothing new in the last essay, which begins again with John 1.11. The brief introduction is almost poetical in style and ends: 'The heads of Jewish society placed him on the cross. Why did they not understand him?' At the beginning of his comments the writer claims: 'The really important arguments, which also led to his crucifixion, took place with the intellectuals' (by which he means the Sadducees and Pharisees). For the Pharisees 'the law of Moses was by no means sufficient. They supplemented it with many detailed, petty regulations.' In what follows he tries honestly to reconcile his prejudices and the literature consulted with the lectures, the result being that his essay seems inconsistent and incoherent. Thus, after describing the incident of the adulteress (John 8), he writes: 'This passage shows clearly Jesus' criticism of the scribes. They regard them-

140

selves as righteous and condemn the fallen human being without hesitation.' Jesus has to tell them that they are wrong. 'This must have been the supreme insult for a Jew claiming to be faithful to the law.' But again: 'Jesus certainly did not completely scorn the Pharisees [Matt. 23.1–3]. For they also occupied an important place in the people's lives and did much for religion.' The Pharisee, however, comes off very badly when compared with the publican (Luke 8.9–14). And the writer refers at length to the condemnation of the Pharisees and scribes in the different Gospels. The essay presents a good example of how difficult it is—almost impossible—to fight against ideas accepted for centuries. To the Samaritan woman at the well (John 4) Jesus says clearly that he is the Messiah. As opposed to the Jews, the Samaritans believe in him. We can only hope that these students with their naïve-fundamentalist view of the Gospel accounts have been better instructed in the course of their later studies. But would it not then have been too late to eradicate the deeply rooted prejudices which these more or less mature individuals—they would then be at least twenty-four and many considerably older—had brought with them, particularly as they would find these prejudices continually confirmed afresh in the relevant literature?

In this last essay the description of the social conditions in the country is completely without foundation: 'From the religious standpoint, poverty was regarded as a real stain, since people were all too ready to see poverty and sin as interdependent.' Apparently the writer knows nothing of the poverty of some of the most respected rabbis in the country. 'The Jews were likewise far from accepting the emancipation of women. Women were allowed to enter only the forecourt of the temple. . . . The way in which a young girl was married off by her parents was degrading by our standards.' Evidently he learned nothing from his sources about the fact that the position of women in Judaism was far more secure than in other nations at the time. It seems as if this student had picked up opinions on the conditions in Palestine indiscriminately wherever he could find them, put them together, and drew the conclusion: Jesus 'was a genuine man of God. . . . At one

141

time they [the people] wanted to make him king. But the cry "Hosanna" fades out. On Good Friday it becomes "Crucify him! Not this man, but Barabbas".'

The echo of the literature discussed at length in the previous chapters could be heard again without difficulty in all these essays. As long as authoritative scholars describe Judaism in the way we have shown, it is not surprising to find the same views expressed more naively and crudely by students. In fact it could be observed that the anti-Judaism of the latter became stronger, the greater the amount of reading they had done. Lectures by individual teachers with different opinions are of little or no avail against these fixed ideas.

If we are ever to reach a fresh, unbiased approach to Judaism, what is absolutely necessary is a resolution on the part of Old and New Testament scholars to examine afresh their own attitudes and *objectively* to present Jewish teaching and the Jewish way of life between the two Testaments in the light of their study of the *original* Jewish sources and not at second hand (for example, as drawn from the Strack/Billerbeck commentary). To reconcile this presentation then with the statements of the gospel is a great but not impossible task of hermeneutics which is already being attempted by some individuals. And this is a sign of hope for the future.

7

A Short Survey of Anglo-American Authors

This book was meant to be a pilot project, which might inspire some German theologians to undertake a more profound and extensive study. This chapter, added for the English edition, contains a limited survey of some of those writings which are most likely to be consulted by first-year students of theology and Scripture in Britain and the United States. It would be presumptuous to base any firm conclusions on the relatively few authors selected; yet the impression that the attitude to Judaism of Anglo-American authors is different seems justifiable. To establish this conclusion firmly would need a further detailed investigation.

The survey here could only include recent and easily accessible publications. The divisions are the same as for the main part of the book but instead of in a full chapter each topic is dealt with in a few paragraphs only.

Late Judaism and Jewish Religious Community (Kultgemeinde)

It was difficult to find any mention of these concepts. On the whole, the idea is, if not totally absent, hardly ever expressed in terms of a degenerate Judaism rejected in favour of the 'New Israel'. Kee and Young write about two concepts which, in the first century, were basic in popular Jewish thought. 'The first expectation ... was for the coming of an ideal ruler who would establish a reign of righteousness and peace throughout the world ... This expectation obviously implied that the Jewish nation would regain the political prestige it had once enjoyed, but its ultimate meaning was that the nation's resurgence would vindicate the faith of the Jews and the righteousness of God. The second expectation was that God himself would establish his heavenly rule throughout all the world.'[1] Here Jews are always considered a 'nation', and, contrary to the German material, the expectation of the Kingdom of God included the whole world and only as a corollary the 'political prestige' of the Jewish people.

The continuity of past and present Jewish history is implied in the *Jerome Biblical Commentary*: 'The defeat of the Jews in the Second Revolt sealed their fate for 1800 years. Until 1967 they were not masters of the ancient holy city and Temple area ... He [Simon ben Kosibah] was the last major Palestinian political leader whom the Jews had until modern times.'[2] The implications are that Kosibah and General Dayan, separated by 1800 years, are leaders of the same nation, a nation that has always considered Palestine its homeland.

G. E. Ladd admits that he depends on the German Bultmann when he speaks of the rejection of Israel as the people of God and the substitution of a new people. He adds, however, that 'possibly the form of the language of this saying (Mk. 12,9; Mt. 21,43) has been modified by tradition'.[3] Outspokenly anti-Jewish is the Catholic Alexander Jones. His book on Matthew is not a work of serious scholarship but had great popular appeal in the sixties: 'The very refusal of its Messiah by Israel is no break with the past but rather the climax of its melancholy history: Israel's response to God's invitation was never generous [23.35], and Matthew's readers ... need not be surprised nor scandalized that their own nation as a body has rejected the new offer [23.34].'[4]

These few quotations go some way to indicate that English-speaking authors are less preoccupied with 'Late Judaism', nor do they think it necessary to exalt Christianity at the expense of a decadent Judaism. John Marsh puts it succinctly, 'Christianity was cradled in Judaism',[5] and it would seem neither logical nor flattering that a degenerate, obsolete Judaism should have given birth to the Christian faith.

The almost total absence of the 'Late Judaism' concept may

144

be at least partially explained by the fact that, instead of Schürer and Strack/Billerbeck, English-speaking scholars are familiar with the works of R. Travers Herford[6] and G. Foot Moore[7]. Even first-year students, and much more so their professors, would know something of the real values of modern Judaism, for there exist a steadily increasing literature by Jewish scholars in both countries and flourishing, extremely articulate Jewish communities. All this has been virtually absent in Germany since the nineteen-thirties and partly accounts for the difference in the academic treatment of Judaism.

Law and Legalistic Piety

In *Invitation to the New Testament* by one of the greatest living Scripture scholars, W. D. Davies, the definition of Law is inspired by his first-hand knowledge of Judaism and quite contrary to the German: 'It must be emphasized that the translation of the Hebrew word *Torah* by the English word *Law* has been doubly unfortunate. 'Torah' is a far wider term than the English 'Law'; it stands for direction, teaching, instruction of a religious and moral kind. Indeed, it stands for what we call 'revelation'—the totality of God's will as revealed. It always retains a reference to law or commandment, but it is never exhausted in these terms.'[8] This has become almost a commonplace among English-speaking scholars, though it is doubtful if it has filtered down to the pastors' Sunday sermons. Davies' definition is strictly true; it takes into account the Hebrew root of the term.

D. E. Nineham gives a concrete instance of how mistakes about the Law have occurred in Christian exegesis. He takes the much quoted and rather obscure passage on *Qorban* (Mark 7.10–13). 'The Law made it unmistakably clear that children had a solemn duty to support their parents, but apparently some Jews were avoiding the duty ... The practice was clearly a disgraceful evasion of the demands of the Law ... but it must be added at once that according to the *Mishnah* the rabbis themselves said so very emphatically.' Nineham has obviously consulted the sources, for he adds that, though the passage is somewhat unclear, 'according to the best authorities it means that if a vow prevented a man from supporting his parents, it was right for him to break this vow'.[9] The author then discusses the possibility of a contemporary scandalous case of this nature which might have been the occasion for this passage. All that is in the Gospels is therefore not 'gospel' and has to be carefully evaluated in the light of authentic Jewish sources; the Gospels do not aim at giving an objective account of Jewish practice and teaching.

Much on the same lines is J. C. Fenton, another author of the much consulted *Pelican New Testament Commentaries*. He talks about rewards and punishment and of the custom of ascribing to Judaism the idea that fulfilment of a law necessarily brought a reward and that observance was therefore external and 'legalistic'. But reward and punishment, he continues, are very frequently mentioned in the New Testament: 'Indeed, we might contrast the New Testament unfavourably, in this respect, with one of the Jewish rabbis, who said, "Be not like servants who serve their lord on condition of receiving a reward; but rather be like servants who serve their lord under no condition of receiving a reward" (*Pirqe Aboth* 1.3).'[10]

Norman Perrin's insight is similar: 'The Old Testament has at its heart not a law to be fulfilled in order that man may achieve righteousness in the sight of God, but a gospel to which men respond and by responding enter into a dynamic relationship with their redeemer; this dynamic relationship is "life" (Deut. 30,15,19).'[11] He adds that 'although mixed with a more "legalistic" understanding' it was this 'conception of Law as response to the saving activity of God' which constituted the essence of the Old Testament concept of Law. This explains 'why the Law always remained a joy and a privilege and never a burden, even to the rabbis with their developed "legalism"'.[12] This is a long way from the German understanding of and contempt for the Law and from the artificial dichotomy between Law and Grace. Far from being mutually exclusive the two complement each other, as is made quite clear in a number of passages in St John's Gospel, for instance 14.21.

There are less positive but still objective investigations into the meaning of Law, for example by T. W. Manson.[13] He reasons that any law is, to begin with, so general that it needs detailed, ongoing interpretation; this happened not only with the Jewish law but with the religious and civil law in all countries. The difference, for him, between Jewish teaching and that of Jesus was that the rabbis always had in mind the community, for which legislation is necessary to avoid chaos, while Jesus is concerned with the individual response to a personal call. Though less sympathetic than the above quoted authors, this writer too makes a real effort to understand the reasons behind Jewish 'legalism' and tries to explain it without facile prejudice.

On the whole, and keeping in mind that these are only a few examples, the impression is of a sincere attempt to do justice to a concept crucial to Judaism. The customary extreme positions—here the rigour of the Law, there the teaching of love and grace—have given way to unbiased research. Law, love, and grace have their place in both Judaism and Christianity. These concepts do not constitute the great divide! There is room here for a further study of the Pauline concept of the Law which does not correspond to authentic Jewish teaching but, possibly, to a personal experience.[14]

The Pharisees and Scribes

When one investigates the definition of Pharisees and scribes one meets with a certain ambivalence: some authors cannot go beyond the Gospel accounts, others are more sensitive to the historical background of the final editing of the Gospels and/or get their portrait from Jewish sources. J. C. Fenton's *The Gospel of St Matthew* puts this succinctly when he discusses the much quoted 'Woes' (ch. 23): 'There are two points which the reader should bear in mind in this chapter. First, the experts on the Judaism of the first century tell us that the Scribes and Pharisees have been considerably caricatured here, they were not at all like this picture of them, indeed many were extremely loving and holy men. Second, the warnings against the Scribes and Pharisees are not meant to be taken as just warnings against those particular men ... but as a portrait of unbelief at any time, anywhere. The scope of this chapter is much wider than it might at first seem: it is addressed to the Church ... The Scribes and Pharisees are used as lay-figures, or representatives of practical atheism which masquerades as piety. The reader may feel that Matthew has been severe and cold in his condemnation of the Jewish leaders; and we are told that in fact he has misrepresented them. Matthew's defence of what he has done might well be to repeat Nathan's words (to David), "You are the man".'[15]

This long quotation is representative of a whole hermeneutical trend in Anglo-American exegesis; it makes the Gospel relevant for today; it is the reader today who is addressed. Moreover, as subsequent quotes will show, the Matt. 23 passage can only be fully understood in the context of the situation in which the young Christian community found itself vis-à-vis the Synagogue after the year A.D. 70. Thus G. B. Caird comments on the similar passage in *The Gospel of Luke* (11.37–54): 'The Woes ... are a collection made by the compiler of Q, perhaps for use in the continuing debate between Church and Synagogue.'[16]

The Jerome Biblical Commentary tries to reconcile a negative and a positive view: 'After the destruction of Jerusalem ... it gave them [the Pharisees] the advantage of a rallying point for the Jews. It is the Pharisaic tradition that molded the Judaism which survived after that catastrophe ... But the *separatism* of the Pharisees induced in some of them a haughty pride and withdrawal from the "rabble that knows not the Law". It was this attitude that caused Jesus of Nazareth to castigate the Pharisees severely (Matt. 23), although it must be admitted that the Gospel evaluation of the Pharisees, since it emerged from an apologetic context, is far too negative and does not give the Pharisees sufficient credit for being a constructive spiritual force.'[17]

John Reumann firmly adopts this last outlook to situate the Gospel portrait of the Pharisees in its historical context: 'After A.D. 70 when the temple was destroyed, there were no more priests; it was the Pharisees and rabbis who constituted, and hence were identified with, the Jewish opposition to Christianity. The long tirade in Matthew 23 against the "Scribes and Pharisees" ... doubtless reflects the changed situation. It is a fact that in some of the controversy stories ... the Pharisees' criticisms are directed against the followers of Jesus—and hence against the early Christians—rather than against Jesus himself (see Mk. 2:18,24).'[18]

As all the authors consulted mention the Pharisees it would take many pages to quote each one. To make clear what is meant by the ambivalent attitude only two more passages will be cited. These show that there is real struggle, even within one and the same author, to reconcile historical, objective knowledge of Pharisaism and the Gospel accounts. W. D. Davies offers such an instance. In his *Invitation* he does justice to the Pharisees as they appear in non-Christian sources. The Pharisees, he writes, 'accepted as axiomatic that the divine will was revealed in the Law and that every aspect of human life is to be governed by the Law. But the Pharisees also recognized that no written document can cover every detail of life. Changing conditions demand not an immutable code but a living, adaptable one. The Pharisees, therefore, claimed that, in addition to the written Law, the Oral Law had authority. Moreover, they were in favour of adapting the Law more and more to make it relevant to their times ... Within Judaism, the Pharisees were what we should call today "liberals"—men anxious to make religion living, vital, contemporary.'[19] But when it comes to commenting on the Gospel itself, the attitude changes. Speaking of the healing of the man born blind (John 9), Professor Davies writes, 'The Pharisees call good evil and evil good; they refuse to rejoice generously in the healing activity of Jesus. They consider him a commonplace fellow of unknown origin.'[20] In fairness one must mention that he alludes to the Church-Synagogue conflict of the late first century, the date of the editing of this Gospel. 'John was writing at a time when the Christian Church was increasingly being estranged from the Synagogue.'[21]

A similar ambiguity is noticeable in the following last instance from *The Living World of the New Testament*: 'So although on the one hand the Oral Torah brought religious faith and practice nearer to the average Jew ... on the other hand the elaborate rules of the Pharisees cut them off from many of their fellow Jews. Their attitude inevitably brought with it the danger of self-righteousness, a danger that they repeatedly combatted in their writings.'[22] Thus, as far as the Pharisees are concerned, the attitude is almost schizophrenic. Considered by themselves, the Pharisees are pious men, concerned with doing and teaching the revealed will of God. When, however, the Pharisees are portrayed as the opponents of Jesus in the controversy stories of the Gospels, their teaching must contain some basic defect, because it blinds them to the person of Jesus. Even the apparently unbiased scholar, one with as especially profound knowledge of Jewish sources as W. D. Davies, finds it difficult to admit that a pious Pharisee could, in good faith, not recognize in Jesus the one they were expecting and for whose sake they should give up their most precious patrimony, the word of God in the Torah.

Jewish Guilt in the Death of Jesus

The English exegetical literature on this topic is, with a very few exceptions and always remembering the brevity of this survey, of one mind. The Jewish opposition to Jesus was a sincerely held conviction, and Jewish 'guilt' is thereby much attenuated. Moreover, Pilate is as much, if not more to blame than the Jewish leaders, despite the whitewashing process which begins with Mark and reaches a climax first in John, then in the apocryphical literature; the Coptic Church has even canonized him.

D. E. Nineham's excellent commentary on Mark investigates the trial before the Sanhedrin: 'The possibility cannot be ruled out that 14:53–65 is mainly a deduction by the early Christians ... Certainly the early Christians were regarded by their Jewish contemporaries as blasphemers for proclaiming as Messiah one who had been crucified ... the idea could therefore easily have arisen that if it was blasphemy for the Christians to claim Messiahship for the crucified Christ, it must have been blasphemy to have made the same claim for himself.'[23]

Already in John, as later in the Church fathers, the 'Jews were seen by the Christians as having deliberately rejected Christ in full knowledge of his claims and the evidence in their support'.[24] This seems to us today an untenable position. The question, as Nineham continues, is complex; all evidence points to the fact that most Jews who came in contact with Jesus alive, and particularly after the crucifixion, could honestly not recognize in him the one they expected. It is not much help to point to the miracles—Greek as well as Jewish miracle workers were not unknown at the time. Principally, however, Jesus did not fulfil the prophetic expectations of a Messiah ushering in the kingdom of God visibly and universally. It is a general mistake to suppose these expectations to have been merely national and materialistic. Certainly they included the ingathering of diaspora Jewry in their homeland and the end of pagan rule in Palestine, but they foretold first and foremost the worship of the one true God by all nations and the cessation of war, disease, and injustice, and Jesus was not that kind of Messiah. It does not help to adduce here the resurrection; this is not a proof but an object of faith, accepted by those who already believe.

As for apportioning the blame to Pilate and/or the Jewish leaders, Nineham writes: 'The experience of the Church, especially after A.D. 70, was that while the Jews increasingly refused to accept Christ's claims, the Romans were sometimes surprisingly friendly and Gentiles in general seemed much more inclined to believe. It was therefore natural to lay the blame for the crucifixion exclusively on the Jews and to exonerate the Romans completely.'[25] Nineham is very strong on this point and returns to it several times: 'As St Mark presents it, the story ... has the effect of concealing what must have been the fact, that a Roman judge formally condemned Jesus as a criminal and of throwing the responsibility for Jesus' death almost entirely on the Jews.'[26] The author gives an historically objective portrait of Pilate, idealized beyond recognition in the Gospels.

Nineham's views are contradicted by one of his colleagues, G. B. Caird, the commentator in the same Pelican series on

St Luke: 'There is a savage irony in the threefold accusation that he [Jesus] is an insurgent leader who has been inciting the people to disaffection against Rome and laying claim to royal status. His accusers know very well that it is precisely because he had refused to be this kind of Messiah that his own nation has rejected him. The charge is a deliberate and malicious inversion of the truth. Pilate has enough sagacity to see through their duplicity.'[27] This, together with Alexander Jones' commentary on St Matthew, is the only totally negative comment on the 'guilt' of the Jews. Jones, after comparing Pilate's pagan wife favourably to the Jews—the author takes this much disputed passage literally!—continues: 'It is before God and not before Tiberius that the Jews take responsibility upon themselves and their descendants'[28] for Jesus' death.

Even William Barclay, whose writings tend to show an ambivalent portrait of the Jews, says, 'Jesus died because of the enmity of the leaders of orthodox Judaism'[29] (the use of the term 'orthodox' for first-century Jewry shows how little acquainted the author is with the situation in Palestine); however, he precedes this by explaining: 'Their enmity was not an embittered or small-minded thing; it was born of the genuine conviction that the teaching and example of Jesus were destructive of all true religion.'[30] If a trial before the Sanhedrin did take place at all and if some hastily convoked Jewish authorities condemned Jesus, it is only fair to stress that they might well have been sincere in their conviction that they were faced with another of the several rabble-rousing messianic pretenders of the troubled first century.

W. D. Davies and his fellow scholars understand the sincere dilemma in which Jewry, faced with Jesus' and his followers' messianic claim, found themselves: 'To most, if not all, Jews such a claim could not but be scandalous. It is enough to point to the figure of Jesus of Nazareth as the Messiah, but to point to a crucified Jesus as such was monstrous ... However much a Jew might have been at home in the vocabulary, style, atmosphere and concepts of the Fourth Gospel, he would stumble at the claim that all his great expectations for the future were already offered to him by a figure who died on the cross.

The response of a Jew to such a claim could not but be one of shock.'[31] The way the Churches have emphasized this fulfilment in a world of destructiveness and recurring tragic calamities, coupled with the fate of the Jewish people in a so-called Christian society, cannot have attenuated this reaction of shock and total disbelief.

The Jerome Biblical Commentary on the 'guilt' question is brief and expresses the results of modern scholarship. On Matt. 27.25: ' "All the people answered": Matthew's addition of the acceptance by the Jewish spokesman of the guilt is a theological addition, written with the disaster of the Jewish War in mind; this was seen by the early Christians as a terrible judgement on the people who had secured the killing of their Messiah by the perversion of justice . . . It is scarcely Matthew's thought that the plea of innocence that he puts in the mouth of Pilate (27.24) could be regarded as genuine.'[32] The whole scene is now mostly understood as a theological interpretation and not as an objective historical report. It cannot be emphasized often enough that the Gospels are not biography but *kerygma*, that they were finally edited in a particular historical situation of conflict between Church and Synagogue, and that they reflect this situation.

Though John Marsh's commentary on St John shows traces of the older condemnatory judgements, for instance of the Pharisees, he is all the same able to distinguish between fact and a late writer's intention: 'John is perhaps more concerned than the Synoptics to expose the heavy burden of guilt resting upon "The Jews", by which he means primarily the chief priests and scribes.'[33] He goes further: 'What the story shows is that the crucifixion of Jesus Christ was not the result of an alliance between men motivated wholly by vicious inclinations; it is rather that good men are driven to evil sometimes by the very soundness of their intentions.'[34] This author, like some others, is faced by the dilemma of reconciling the Gospel accounts with present-day knowledge of Judaism. They wish to accept the Gospel fully, yet are forced to question its reports in the light of modern scholarship.

Here, to end with, are two American comments, among the

most recent and outspoken. John Reumann begins by pointing out how often the concept of Jewish 'guilt' has been the cause of anti-Semitism and also contributed to the Nazi persecution. He then examines the whitewashing of Pilate in the Gospels and later writings. But he goes on with a positive explanation of the events leading to the crucifixion: 'For the New Testament, especially for Paul's theology, the ground of Calvary is equal and all men stand condemned. It is a terrible perversion of the Gospel that by passing guilt for the cross off onto the Jews one somehow exonerates oneself from sin. It is likewise a travesty of justice to assume that the involvement of a handful of Jews in Jerusalem could condemn all Jews in the world in Jesus' day, let alone all Jews of subsequent generations. The Second Vatican Council wrestled with many unfair stigmatizations of the Jews in Roman Catholicism. Protestants, at least those accustomed to careful historical study of the Bible, have come to see that the New Testament scarcely allows men today to draw facile conclusions about "Jewish guilt", and that the tendency to magnify Jewish responsibility is a later development that scarcely fits the original fact. In view of the centuries of partisan abuse that misunderstandings of the Jewish trial of Jesus have brought about, one concrete resolve that ought to occur to every fair-minded person, let alone every disciple of Jesus of Nazareth, is to make redress for false hatreds of the past. The Passion story is no invitation to anti-Semitism, even though some Jews were involved in Jesus' death. For so, too, were some Romans.'[35]

In this passage the author keeps in mind the historical consequences of the biased interpretation of the Gospel texts of the trial. There existed, and still exists, the tendency to use 'the Jews' as a scapegoat, to identify the Christian with the Good Thief, with Mary and John at the foot of the cross, 'the Jews' with the high priests and the bloodthirsty crowd in the Judgement Hall. Comments on the New Testament, especially preaching and teaching, do not occur in a vacuum; they create an attitude if not of hatred, at least of prejudice against a community of people living today in our midst and, according even to the sixteenth-century Catechism of Trent,[36] less guilty of the Passion than the Christian who pretends to believe but does not act according to his faith.

The widely read *Living World of the New Testament* makes an excellent attempt at an all-round picture of what happened at the trial of the Sanhedrin: 'In the eyes of the religious authorities, his [Jesus'] attitude towards the Law and the Temple had already brought their condemnation. He clearly represented a threat to the unity of the people as they conceived it, for to destroy the Law and to belittle the Temple was to threaten the life stream of the Jews. As such, he was threatening not only the nation but God himself. Only when we remember the background of the hearing can we understand the action and reaction of the religious authorities. It was far more than any one statement of Jesus that brought the charge of blasphemy against him.'[37] This seems more probable than the report of the trial in Luke, where Jesus is supposed to have been asked the highly unlikely question: 'Are you the son of God, then?' (22.70). Not only certain incidents in the life of Jesus but even more so the later actions of his disciples—without taking Acts too literally—deserved the accusation of blasphemy with a consequent exclusion from the Synagogue.

The same authors' remark on Pilate only confirms what every unbiased New Testament scholar has discovered: 'According to Mark, Pilate was reluctant to condemn Jesus. There are also other passages in the Synoptics that stress Pilate's reluctance, but they have no foundation in fact. Instead, they developed out of the church's later attempt to lay the blame for Jesus' death on the Jews and to exonerate Rome.'[38]

The interest of the above quotations lies in the fact that almost each scholar strives, more or less successfully, to get at the objective truth. There is less of an *a priori* bias towards an interpretation unfavourable to Jews than in German and French exegesis. The approach to the Gospels is more critical and less literal; there is also a better knowledge of Jewish sources and, most importantly, a consciousness of a living Jewish community to whom an injustice has been done by accusing them of a crime which was due to a sincere politico-religious zeal and to a real, not pretended, ignorance as to the person of Jesus.

From Generation to Generation

During a year's teaching at an American university the present writer gave a course on Judaism which met with an unexpected success. The group of students became enthusiastically involved. They wrote a number of excellent papers on different Jewish topics. The course was not obligatory and none of the students majored in theology. They asked to visit a synagogue and took part in the Friday night liturgy, meeting the congregation afterwards for an informal lively discussion. They also proposed a rapid course in basic Hebrew, which they found difficult but followed through to the final examination. After six years the students have still remained in touch with their lecturer and among one another. Their interest in things Jewish has lasted. Their attitude was open, sympathetic, and absolutely free from any trace of anti-Judaism. It is only fair to add that the socio-political situation in the United States is very different from that in Germany, where—consciously or not—the past is still a problem. The American faculty of theology had two rabbis on the staff, and their lectures, though not compulsory, were crowded. It so happened that there were hardly any Jews at this Catholic university, but this absence only stimulated the desire to meet members of the Jewish community. This was a long way from the almost apathetic response of the German students; special courses in Judaism were proposed several times but only one student was interested—a Japanese!

It would need a far more broadly based study to go into all the reasons for the difference in the scholarly writings as well as the response of the students. If this brief survey could stimulate further research it has more than fulfilled its function.

Notes

CHAPTER 1
INTRODUCTION

1   G. F. Moore, 'Christian Writers on Judaism' in *Harvard Theological Review*, 14 July 1921, pp. 191–254.
2   Ibid., p. 198.
3   Ibid., pp. 221–2.
4   Two examples out of many may be quoted: K. H. Rengstorf and S. von Kortzfleisch (ed.), *Kirche und Synagoge*, 2 vols., 1968; W. P. Eckert, M. P. Levinson, and M. Stöhr (ed.), *Jüdisches Volk—gelobtes Land*, 1970.
5   T. Filthaut, editor of *Israel in der christlichen Unterweisung*, 1963, wanted to follow up this brief, superficial presentation with a longer book, but did not manage it. In December 1972 a conference on the closer investigation of the treatment of the Jewish question in Catholic schoolbooks should have taken place; it had to be cancelled at the last moment because of a lack of participants.
6   Emil Schürer, *Geschichte des jüdischen Volkes im Zeitalter Jesu Christi*, 3 vols., Leipzig, 1901–11. The English translation in five volumes published by T. & T. Clark, Edinburgh, 1916–19, has long been out of print, but a revised edition of volume i appeared in 1973 (see Bibliography).
7   H. Kremers, 'Das Judentum im Evangelischen Religionsunterricht' in M. Stöhr (ed.), *Judentum im christlichen Religionsunterricht*, 1972, p. 54.
8   Martin Noth, *The History of Israel*, London and New York, 1960², p. 432. This book, originally published in German in 1950, has gone into several unrevised editions and has been translated into a number of languages.
9   M. Schmaus, *Katholische Dogmatik*, 8 vols., 1963, vol. ii/2, p. 105. It is only right to add that Schmaus in 1969–70 brought out a new two-volume, modernized version of this work on dogmatic theology in which he quotes the Declaration of the Second Vatican Council also on the Jews. What he says here, by comparison with what he wrote seven years earlier, is modified and very much shortened at least in its formulation. But he maintains his original opinion that the 'consummation of the world' cannot come to pass 'before Israel as a whole turns to Christ'. For him, now as in the earlier work, 'the existence of the Jewish people is eschatologically determined. If the Christian sets his hope in the future,

157

this hope must include the hope of the salvation of the Jewish people' (*Der Glaube der Kirche*, i, p. 509).

10 G. Schiwy, *Der Weg ins Neue Testament*, 4 vols., Würzburg, 1965–70, vol. i, p. 69.

11 Georg Fohrer, 'Die Judenfrage und der Zionismus' in *Studien zur alttestamentlichen Theologie und Geschichte, 1949–66*, Berlin, 1969, p. 44.

12 J. Jeremias, *New Testament Theology: The Proclamation of Jesus*, London and New York, 1971 (German original, Gütersloh, 1971), p. 227.

13 H. U. von Balthasar, *Herrlichkeit*, 3 vols., Einsiedeln, 1961–9, vol. iii/2, p. 31.

14 H. U. von Balthasar, *Who is a Christian?*, London, 1968 (German original, Einsiedeln, 1965), pp. 115–16.

15 Penultimate version of the Declaration, 18 November 1964.

16 M. Dibelius, *Jesus*, Philadelphia, 1949, and London, 1963, p. 38.

17 G. Kittel, *Die Judenfrage*, Stuttgart, 1933, p. 73.

18 Ibid p. 74. Kittel was removed from his professorship in Tübingen in 1945 because of his anti-Semitic attitude during the Nazi period.

19 In what follows two points should be noted:

1) It must be stressed once again that only selected authors are cited here. The list might have been extended, but this would have cost more time and energy than the present author could afford. As it is, special attention was given to works consulted by students.

2) When the manuscript of this book was already completed, a short article, 'The Image of Judaism in Recent Books on Jesus', by M. Brocke (of the University of Regensburg) appeared in the *Freiburger Rundbrief* 1972, pp. 50–9. In this article three books were reviewed which are not mentioned here. Brocke comes to the same conclusions as the present author.

CHAPTER 2

'LATE JUDAISM' AND 'JEWISH RELIGIOUS COMMUNITY'

1 Georg Fohrer, *History of Israelite Religion*, Nashville, 1972 and London, 1973, p. 359.

2 Ibid., p. 365.

3 Ibid., p. 287.

4 Georg Fohrer, *Studien*, p. 32.

5 Ibid.

6 Ibid.

7 Ibid., p. 37.

8 Ibid., p. 47.

9 Ibid., p. 49.

10 Hans Werner Bartsch, 'Die Bedeutung Jerusalems für das jüdische Volk und die Stadt unter Besatzung, Materialen zum Nahostkonflikt, 47', *Evangelischer Arbeitskreis Kirche und Israel in Hessen und Nassau*, i.

11 Ibid.

12 Ibid.

13 Ibid., p. 2.
14 Ibid., p. 3.
15 Ibid., p. 4.
16 Werner Förster, *Palestinian Judaism in New Testament Times* (U.S. title *From the Exile to Christ: Historical Introduction to Palestinian Judaism*), tr. G. E. Harris, Edinburgh and Philadelphia, 1964, pp. 3–4.
17 Ibid., p. 4.
18 Ibid., p. 191.
19 M. Metzger, *Grundriss der Geschichte Israels*, Neukirchen, 1967, p. 215.
20 Ibid., p. 212.
21 G. Schiwy, *Weg* vol. i, pp. 87–8.
22 J. Leipoldt and W. Grundmann (ed.), *Umwelt des Urchristentums*, 3 vols., Berlin, 1965, vol. i, p. 217.
23 E. Lohse, *Israel und die Christenheit*, Göttingen, 1960, p. 34.
24 Romano Guardini, *The Lord*, London, New York, and Toronto, 1956, p. 169.
25 Ibid., p. 99.
26 Ibid.
27 Martin Noth, *The Laws in the Pentateuch and Other Studies*, Edinburgh and London, 1966, and Philadelphia, 1967, p. 63.
28 Ibid., p. 67.
29 Ibid., p. 82.
30 Ibid., p. 83.
31 Martin Noth, *History*, p. 448.
32 Ibid.
33 Ibid., p. 453.
34 Ibid., p. 454.
35 Ibid., p. 432.
36 R. Bultmann, 'Prophecy and Fulfilment' in Claus Westermann (ed.), *Essays on Old Testament Interpretation*, London and Richmond, Virginia, 1963, p. 70.
37 Bultmann, *Theology of the New Testament*, vol. i, London and New York, 1952, pp. 12–13.
38 Ibid., p. 25.
39 W. Grundmann, *Die Geschichte Jesu Christi*, Berlin, 1963³, p. 88.
40 Ibid., p. 112.
41 M. Dibelius, *Jesus*, p. 39.
42 Ibid., p. 40.
43 Günther Bornkamm, *Jesus of Nazareth*, London and New York, 1960, p. 37.
44 Ibid.
45 Leonhard Goppelt, *Jesus, Paul and Judaism*, tr. and ed. Edward Schroeder, New York, 1964, p. 20. (This volume represents the first half of *Christentum und Judentum im ersten und zweiten Jahrhundert: ein Aufriss der Urgeschichte der Kirche*, Gütersloh, 1954.) Future page references, unless otherwise noted, are to this English edition.
46 Ibid., p. 21.

47 Ibid.
48 Ibid., p. 25.
49 Ibid., p. 26.
50 Ibid., p. 22, n. 1 (German edn).
51 Ibid., p. 52.
52 Ibid., p. 93.
53 Ibid., p. 95.
54 Ibid., p. 311 (German edn).
55 Ibid., pp. 312–13 (German edn).
56 Ibid., p. 314 (German edn).
57 M. Schmaus, *Katholische Dogmatik*, vol. ii/2, p. 511.
58 Ibid., p. 513.
59 E. Stauffer, *New Testament Theology*, London and New York, 1955, p. 189.
60 W. G. Kümmel, 'Die Gottesverkündigung Jesu und der Gottesgedanke des Spätjudentums' in *Judaica* i (31 March 1945), pp. 40–68 (quotation p. 52).
61 Ibid., p. 68.
62 W. Bousset and H. Gressmann, *Die Religion des Judentums im späthellenistischen Zeitalter*, Tübingen, 1926, p. 59.
63 Ibid., p. 85.
64 Ibid., p. 96.
65 Ibid., p. 421.
66 Ibid., p. 472.
67 E. Meyer, *Ursprung und Anfänge des Christentums*, Berlin, 3 vols., 1921, p. 437. Bousset is given as the source.
68 Alfred Bertholet, *A History of Hebrew Civilisation*, London, 1926, p. 374.
69 Ibid.
70 Emil Schürer, *Geschichte*, vol. ii, p. 408.
71 Ibid.
72 Ibid., p. 410, n. 50.
73 Ibid., p. 427.
74 M.-J. Lagrange, *Le Messianisme chez les Juifs*, Paris, 1909, p. 276.
75 M.-J. Lagrange, *Le Judaisme avant Jésus-Christ*, Paris, 1931. p. x.
76 Ibid., p. 433.
77 Ibid., p. 479.
78 J. Bonsirven, *Le Judaisme Palestinien au temps de Jésus-Christ*, 2 vols., Paris, 1934–5, vol. ii, p. 200.
79 Ibid., p. 314.

CHAPTER 3

LAW AND LEGALISTIC PIETY

1 Norbert Lohfink, 'Law and Grace' in *The Christian Meaning of the Old Testament*, Milwaukee, 1968, and London, 1969.
2 J. Jeremias, *New Testament Theology*, p. 210.
3 The work of H. L. Strack and P. Billerbeck, constantly used by all

biblical scholars, has been mentioned several times. This is the *Kommentar zum Neuen Testament aus Talmud und Midrasch*, 5 vols., Munich, 1922–8, to which a list of Scripture/scholars and a geographical register, ed. J. Jeremias and K. Adolph, 1961, has been added. This recent date is evidence of the esteem which this selection of Jewish sources continues to enjoy, although it is anything but objective. We would certainly be right in assuming that most Christian authors derive their knowledge of Jewish sources from this monumental work, and this means that it must be blamed for the many false and one-sided pieces of information and conclusions. Here we need mention only one example: Matt. 5.43 on love of neighbour and hatred for enemies. The conclusion drawn by the authors, despite protracted discussion and study of the sources, is a typical example of their procedure in almost every case: 'The first part of the saying comes from Leviticus 19.18; the second cannot be substantiated from the sources. The whole will be a popular maxim used by the average Israelite in Jesus' time to guide his behaviour towards friend and foe' (vol. i, p. 353). There is nothing to be said about pseudo-scholarly logic.

4 J. Jeremias, *New Testament Theology*, p. 147.
5 Ibid.
6 Ibid., p. 148.
7 Ibid., p. 151.
8 Hans Werner Bartsch, *Bedeutung*, p. 3.
9 Georg Fohrer, *Studien*, p. 32.
10 Ibid., p. 42.
11 Ibid., p. 43.
12 Ibid., p. 45.
13 Ibid., p. 46.
14 Ibid.
15 Ibid., p. 53.
16 Ibid.
17 Georg Fohrer, *History*, p. 288.
18 Ibid.
19 Ibid.
20 Ibid.
21 Ibid., p. 362.
22 Ibid.
23 H. Braun, *Jesus*, Stuttgart, 1972³, pp. 23–4.
24 Ibid., pp. 24–5.
25 Ibid., p. 25.
26 Ibid., p. 26.
27 Andrea van Dülmen, *Die Theologie des Gesetzes bei Paulus*, Stuttgart, 1968, p. 220.
28 Ibid., p. 221.
29 Ibid., p. 222.
30 Ibid., p. 223.
31 Ibid.

32 G. Schiwy, *Weg*, vol. iii, p. 78.
33 Ibid., pp. 78–9.
34 Werner Förster, *Palestinian Judaism*, pp. 5–6.
35 Ibid., p. 7.
36 Ibid., p. 219.
37 M. Metzger, *Gundriss*, p. 238.
38 G. Schiwy, *Weg*, vol. i, p. 69.
39 Ibid., p. 73.
40 Ibid.
41 J. Leipoldt and W. Grundmann (ed.), *Umwelt*, vol. i, p. 233.
42 Ibid., p. 274.
43 Romano Guardini, *The Lord*, p. 169.
44 Ibid., p. 170.
45 J. Jeremias, *The Parables of Jesus*, London and New York, 1963, p. 139.
46 H. Schlier, *Die Zeit der Kirche*, Freiburg, 1976, p. 46.
47 Ibid., p. 239.
48 Ibid.
49 Ibid., p. 240.
50 W. Grundmann, *Geschichte*, p. 87.
51 Ibid., p. 116.
52 Ibid., p. 124.
53 Ibid.
54 Ibid., p. 138.
55 Martin Noth, *Laws*, p. 106.
56 Ibid., p. 107.
57 E. Lohse, *Israel*, p. 15.
58 Ibid., p. 22.
59 Ibid., p. 23.
60 M. Dibelius, *Jesus*, p. 104.
61 Ibid.
62 Ibid., p. 109.
63 Ibid., p. 117.
64 Paul Tillich, *Systematic Theology*, vol. ii, London, 1957, pp. 93–4.
65 Günther Bornkamm, *Jesus*, p. 40.
66 Ibid., p. 104.
67 R. Bultmann, 'Prophecy' p. 74.
68 R. Bultmann, *Theology*, vol. i, p. 11.
69 Ibid., p. 17.
70 Leonhard Goppelt, *Jesus, Paul and Judaism*, p. 38.
71 Ibid., p. 64.
72 Ibid., pp. 155–6.
73 Ibid., p. 156.
74 *Theological Dictionary of the New Testament*, Grand Rapids, Michigan, vol. iv, 1967, p. 1043.
75 Ibid., p. 1055.
76 Ibid., p. 1083–4. At some points in the article there is evidence of an

attempt to do justice to the Jewish conception of the law.

77 Erik Peterson, *Die Kirche aus Juden und Heiden*, Salzburg, 1933, p. 26.
78 W. Bousset and H. Gressmann, *Religion des Judentums*, p. 85.
79 Ibid, p. 100.
80 Ibid., p. 101.
81 Ibid., p. 117.
82 Ibid., p. 133.
83 Ibid., p. 136.
84 Ibid., p. 298.
85 Ibid., p. 372.
86 Ibid., p. 409.
87 Ibid.
88 Ibid., p. 416.
89 Adolf von Harnack, *Marcion*, Leipzig, 1921, p. 250.
90 A. Schlatter, *Die Geschichte des Christus*, Stuttgart, 1923, p. 364.
91 Ibid., p. 444.
92 E. Meyer, *Ursprung*, vol. ii, p. 428.
93 Ibid., p. 429.
94 Ibid., p. 431.
95 Ibid., p. 427.
96 Alfred Bertholet, *History*, p. 374.
97 Ibid., p. 378.
98 Ibid., pp. 378–9.
99 J. Wellhausen, *Israelitische und jüdische Geschichte*, Berlin, 1914, p. 282.
100 Ibid., p. 283.
101 Ibid., p. 284.
102 Ibid., p. 364.
103 Emil Schürer, *Geschichte*, vol. ii, p. 364.
104 Ibid., p. 372.
105 Ibid., p. 489.
106 Ibid., p. 499.
107 Ibid., p. 545.
108 Ibid.
109 Ibid., pp. 545–6.
110 Ibid., p. 546.
111 Ibid., p. 547.
112 Ibid., p. 569.
113 Ibid., p. 572.
114 Ibid., p. 577.
115 Ibid., p. 579.
116 M.-J. Lagrange, *Messianisme*, p. 297.
117 M.-J. Lagrange, *Judaisme*, p. 479.
118 J. Bonsirven, *On the Ruins of the Temple*, London, 1931, p. 275.
119 J. Bonsirven, *Judaisme*, vol. ii, p. 68.
120 Ibid., pp. 313–14.
121 Ibid., p. 317.

122 Pierre Benoit, *Jesus and the Gospel*, vol. ii, London, 1973, p. 34.
123 Ibid.

CHAPTER 4
PHARISEES AND SCRIBES

1   J. Jeremias, *New Testament Theology*, p. 151.
2   Ibid., p. 146.
3   Ibid.
4   Ibid., p. 147.
5   Ibid.
6   Ibid., pp. 147–8.
7   Ibid., p. 148.
8   Ibid.
9   Ibid., p. 147.
10 H. Braun, *Jesus*, p. 18.
11 Ibid., p. 125.
12 Georg Fohrer, *Studien*, p. 45.
13 Werner Förster, *Palestinian Judaism*, p. 171.
14 Ibid., p. 174.
15 Ibid., p. 175.
16 Ibid., p. 214.
17 M. Metzger, *Grundriss*, pp. 185–6.
18 Ibid., p. 218.
19 Ibid.
20 J. Leipoldt and W. Grundmann (ed.),*Umwelt*, vol. i, p. 277.
21 Ibid., p. 439.
22 G. Schiwy, *Weg*, vol. i, p. 23.
23 Ibid., p. 73.
24 Ibid., p. 75.
25 Ibid., p. 159.
26 Ibid., pp. 160–1.
27 Bo Reicke, *The New Testament Era*, London, 1969 and Philadelphia, 1968, p. 157.
28 Ibid., p. 159.
29 Ibid.
30 Ibid., p. 157.
31 Romano Guardini, *The Lord*, p. 99.
32 Ibid.
33 J. Jeremias, *Jerusalem in the Time of Jesus*, London and Philadelphia, 1969, p. 243.
34 Ibid., p. 247.
35 Ibid., p. 257.
36 Ibid., p. 259.
37 Ibid., p. 263.
38 Ibid., p. 266–7.
39 W. Grundmann, *Geschichte*, p. 112.

Notes

40 Ibid., p. 127.
41 Ibid., p. 109.
42 Ibid., p. 127.
43 Ibid., p. 129.
44 Ibid., p. 131.
45 M. Dibelius, *Jesus*, p. 39.
46 Ibid., p. 116.
47 Paul Tillich, *Systematic Theology*, vol. ii, p. 152.
48 E. Stauffer, *New Testament Theology*, p. 91.
49 Ibid.
50 Ibid., p. 92.
51 Ibid.
52 Ibid., p. 93.
53 Günther Bornkamm, *Jesus*, p. 40.
54 Ibid., p. 104.
55 K. Beyschlag, *Die Bergpredigt und Franz von Assisi*, Gütersloh, 1955, pp. 23–4.
56 Leonhard Goppelt, *Jesus, Paul and Judaism*, p. 58.
57 Ibid., p. 60.
58 Ibid., p. 67.
59 Ibid., p. 68.
60 M. Dibelius, 'The Social Motive in the New Testament', appendix to *Jesus*, p. 154.
61 E. Hänchen, 'Matthäus 23' in *Zeitschrift für katholische Theologie* 48 (1951), pp. 38–63 (quotation, p. 59).
62 Ibid., p. 60.
63 Ibid., pp. 60–1.
64 Ibid., p. 61.
65 W. Bousset and H. Gressmann, *Die Religion des Judentums*, p. 138.
66 Ibid., p. 139.
67 Ibid., p. 168–9.
68 Ibid., p. 184.
69 Ibid.
70 Ibid., p. 185.
71 Ibid., p. 189.
72 Ibid., p. 189 n. 1.
73 G. F. Moore, 'Christian Writers', p. 230.
74 A. Schlatter, *Geschichte*, p. 287.
75 Ibid.
76 Ibid., p. 288.
77 Ibid., p. 299.
78 Ibid., p. 449.
79 Ibid., p. 450.
80 E. Meyer, *Ursprung*, vol. ii, p. 284.
81 Ibid., p. 285.
82 Ibid., p. 295.
83 Ibid., vol. iii, p. 401.

84 J. Wellhausen, *Israelitische und jüdische Geschichte*, p. 283.
85 Ibid., p. 357.
86 Ibid., p. 363.
87 E. Schürer, *Geschichte*, vol. ii, p. 548.
88 Ibid., p. 550.
89 M.-J. Lagrange, *Messianisme*, p. 142.
90 Ibid., p. 144.
91 Ibid., p. 145.
92 M.-J. Lagrange, *Judaisme*, p. 160.
93 Ibid., p. 275.
94 Ibid., p. 294.
95 Joseph Bonsirven, *On the Ruins*, p. 274.
96 P. Benoit, *Jesus and the Gospel*, vol. ii, p. 35, n. 2.
97 Benoit, *Exégèse et Théologie*, Paris, 1961–8, vol. ii, p. 343.

CHAPTER 5
JEWISH GUILT IN THE DEATH OF JESUS

1   J. Jeremias, *New Testament Theology*, Part 1, p. 279. For a full treat-
    ment of this subject, including an exhaustive bibliography, consult
    Gerard S. Sloyan, *Jesus on Trial: The Development of the Passion
    Narratives and Their Historical and Ecumenical Implications*, ed. with an
    introduction by John Reumann (Philadelphia, 1973).
2   Ibid.
3   Ibid., p. 285.
4   J. Blinzler, *The Trial of Jesus*, Westminster, Maryland, 1959, p. 290.
5   Ibid., pp. 290–1.
6   Ibid., p. 291.
7   Ibid.
8   Ibid., p. 292.
9   Ibid.
10 Georg Fohrer, *Studien*, p. 44.
11 Ibid., pp. 44–5.
12 Ibid., pp. 49–50.
13 G. Schiwy, *Weg*, vol. iii, p. 78.
14 Ibid., p. 80.
15 Ibid., pp. 83–4.
16 Leonard Goppelt, *Christologie und Ethik*, Göttingen, 1968, p. 187.
17 Ibid.
18 M. Metzger, *Grundriss*, p. 237.
19 Ibid., p. 218.
20 J. Leipoldt and W. Grundmann (ed.), *Umwelt*, vol. i, p. 439.
21 G. Schiwy, *Weg*, vol. i, p. 162.
22 Ibid., vol. ii, p. 31.
23 Ibid., vol. ii, p. 279.
24 Ibid., p. 158.

Notes

25 Karl Rahner, 'Bekenntnis zu Jesus Christus' in H. J. Schultz (ed.), *Juden, Christen, Deutsche*, 1961, p. 151.
26 Karl Rahner, *Spiritual Exercises*, London, 1967, p. 228.
27 Ibid., pp. 229–30.
28 Ibid., p. 230.
29 Ibid., p. 234.
30 Ibid., p. 235.
31 Ibid., p. 237.
32 H. Schlier, *The Relevance of the New Testament*, London and New York, 1968, p. 216.
33 Ibid., p. 220.
34 Ibid., p. 222.
35 Ibid., p. 223.
36 Ibid., p. 224.
37 Ibid., p. 253.
38 E. Lohse, *History of the Suffering and Death of Jesus Christ*, Philadelphia, 1967, p. 89.
39 Ibid., p. 104.
40 J. Blank, 'Die Gegenwartseschatologie im Johannesevangelium' in K. Schubert (ed.), *Vom Messias zum Christus*, Freiburg, 1964, pp. 305–306.
41 Ibid., p. 306.
42 Ibid., p. 307.
43 Ibid., p. 308.
44 Ibid.
45 Ibid., pp. 309–10.
46 Romano Guardini, *The Lord*, p. 98.
47 Ibid., p. 99.
48 M. Schmaus, *Katholische Dogmatik*, vol. ii/2, p. 105.
49 Ibid., p. 124.
50 Ibid., p. 342.
51 Ibid., p. 511.
52 Ibid., p. 513.
53 Ibid., vol. iii/1, p. 79.
54 Ibid., p. 82.
55 Ibid.
56 Ibid., vol. iii/2, p. 303.
57 Ibid., vol. iv/2, pp. 166–7.
58 Ibid., p. 167.
59 Ibid.
60 Ibid., p. 168.
61 J. Jeremias, *Jerusalem*, p. 267.
62 H. Schlier, *Die Zeit def Kirche*, p. 241.
63 Ibid.
64 Ibid.
65 Ibid., p. 242.
66 Ibid.

67   Ibid., p. 243. It should be added that Schlier is one of the most distinguished modern German Catholic theologians.
68   E. Lohse, *Israel*, p. 20.
69   Ibid., p. 27.
70   Ibid., pp. 62–3.
71   W. Zimmerli, 'Promise and Fulfilment' in Claus Westermann (ed.), *Essays on Old Testament Interpretation*, London and New York, 1963, p. 104.
72   Ibid., p. 114.
73   Ibid., p. 115.
74   Ibid., p. 122.
75   M. Dibelius, *Jesus*, p. 115.
76   Ibid., p. 117.
77   E. Stauffer, *Jesus*, Berne, 1957, p. 64.
78   Ibid., p. 65.
79   Ibid., p. 96.
80   Ibid., p. 98.
81   Ibid., p. 99.
82   Ibid.
83   Ibid., p. 101.
84   Cf. W. Trilling, *Das wahre Israel*, Munich, 1964, pp. 71–2.
85   E. Stauffer, *New Testament Theology*, p. 190.
86   Ibid.
87   E. Stauffer, *Jesus*, p. 9.
88   E. Stauffer, 'Der Prozess Jesu im Oberammergauer Textbuch' in *Völker hörten die signale—Oberammergau Report 70/80*, 1971, p. 29.
89   Ibid., pp. 29–30.
90   Leonhard Goppelt, *Jesus, Paul and Judaism*, p. 93.
91   Ibid., p. 96.
92   Ibid., p. 95, n.3.
93   Ibid., p. 156.
94   Ibid., p. 166.
95   Ibid., p. 167.
96   Ibid., p. 315 (German edn).
97   R. Bultmann, *Theology*, vol. i, p. 21.
98   D. Bonhöffer, 'Die Kirche vor der Judenfrage', lecture, April 1933 in E. Bethge (ed.), *Gesammelte Schriften*, Munich, vol. ii, 1965, pp. 49–50.
99   W. Bousset and H. Gressmann, *Religion*, p. 472.
100 Ibid., p. 524.
101 A. Schlatter, *Geschichte*, p. 182.
102 Ibid., p. 276.
103 Ibid., p. 506.
104 M.-J. Lagrange, *Messianisme*, p. 331.
105 J. Bonsirven, *On the Ruins*, p. 71.
106 Ibid., p. 274.
107 A. Robert and A. Feuillet (ed.), *Introduction to the New Testament*, New York, 1968, p. 800.

Notes

108 Xavier Léon-Dufour (ed.), *Dictionary of Biblical Theology*, London, 1967, p. 242.
109 Ibid., p. 377.
110 Pierre Benoit, *Exégèse*, vol. ii, p. 324.
111 Ibid., p. 325.
112 Ibid.
113 Ibid., p. 325–6.
114 Ibid., p. 326.
115 Ibid., pp. 326–7.
116 Ibid., vol. iii, p. 409.
117 Ibid., p. 110.
118 Ibid.
119 Ibid., p. 411.
120 Ibid., p. 420.
121 Ibid.
122 Ibid., p. 438.

CHAPTER 6
'FROM GENERATION TO GENERATION'

1 M. Stöhr (ed.), *Judaism im christlichen Religionsunterricht*, Frankfurt, 1972, pp. 53–4.
2 The essays are in the possession of the author of the present book. For obvious reasons, no names or other details are given.

CHAPTER 7
A SHORT SURVEY OF ANGLO–AMERICAN AUTHORS

1 H. C. Kee and F. W. Young, *The Living World of the New Testament*, London, 1960 and Englewood Cliffs, New Jersey, 1973, p. 37. The Eng. edn is used here.
2 R. E. Brown, J. A. Fitzmyer and M. E. Murphy, *The Jerome Biblical Commentary*, London and Englewood Cliffs, New Jersey, 1968, 2 vols., vol. ii, p. 702.
3 G. E. Ladd, *Jesus and the Kingdom*, London and New York, 1966, p. 245.
4 Alexander Jones, *The Gospel According to St. Matthew*, London, 1965, pp. 22–3.
5 John Marsh, *The Gospel of St. John*, The Pelican New Testament Commentaries, Harmondsworth, Middx, 1968, p. 172.
6 R. Travers Herford, *The Pharisees*, London, 1924; *Judaism in the New Testament Period*, London, 1928.
7 G. F. Moore, *Judaism*, 3 vols., 1927, 7th edn, 1954.
8 W. D. Davies, *Invitation to the New Testament*, New York, 1966, p. 29.
9 D. E. Nineham, *The Gospel of St. Mark*, The Pelican New Testament Commentaries, Harmondsworth, Middx, 1971, p. 190.
10 J. C. Fenton, *The Gospel of St. Matthew*, The Pelican Gospel Commentaries, Harmondsworth, Middx, 1968, p. 25.

11   Norman Perrin, *The Kingdom of God in the Teaching of Jesus*, London and Philadelphia, 1963, pp. 204–5.
12   Ibid., p. 206.
13   T. W. Manson, *The Teaching of Jesus*, Cambridge, 1955, pp. 296–7.
14   A good study on the question is P. Démann's 'Moise et la Loi dans la pensée de St. Paul', *Cahiers Sioniens* viii, 1954.
15   J. C. Fenton, *Gospel*, pp. 364–5.
16   G. B. Caird, *The Gospel of St. Luke. The Pelican Gospel Commentaries*, Harmondsworth, Middx, 1968, p. 158.
17   *The Jerome Biblical Commentary*, vol. ii, p. 692.
18   John Reumann, *Jesus in the Church's Gospel*, Philadelphia, 1968 and London, 1970, p. 259.
19   W. D. Davies, *Invitation*, pp. 33–4.
20   Ibid., p. 455.
21   Ibid., p. 456.
22   H. C. Kee and F. W. Young, *Living World*, p. 41.
23   D. E. Nineham, *Gospel*, p. 404.
24   Ibid., p. 405.
25   Ibid., pp. 367–8.
26   Ibid., p. 417.
27   G. B. Caird, *Gospel*, p. 246.
28   Alexander Jones, *Gospel*, p. 309.
29   William Barclay, *The First Three Gospels*, London, 1966, p. 179.
30   Ibid., p. 178.
31   W. D. Davies, *Invitation*, pp. 415–16.
32   *Jerome Biblical Commentary*, vol. ii, p. 111.
33   John Marsh, *Gospel*, p. 579.
34   Ibid., p. 606.
35   John Reumann, *Jesus*, p. 67.
36   *Catechism of the Council of Trent for Parish Priests*, Part 1, ch. 5, prg. 11, New York, 1923.
37   H. C. Kee and F. W. Young, *Living World*, p. 172.
38   Ibid.

Select Bibliography

ET = English Translation. Where there is no ET of a German work, an English rendering of the title is given in brackets.

Balthasar, H. U. von, *Martin Buber and Christianity*. London, Harvill, 1961; New York, Macmillan, 1962.
— *Who is a Christian?* London, Burns & Oates; Glen Rock, N.J. Paulist-Newman, 1968.
Barclay, W., *The First Three Gospels*. London, SCM, 1966; Philadelphia, Westminster, 1967.
— *New Testament Words*. London, SCM; Naperville, Ill., Allenson, 1964.
Benoit, P., *Jesus and the Gospel*. 2 vols. New York, McGraw-Hill, 1969; London, Darton, Longman & Todd, 1973.
Bertholet, A., *A History of Hebrew Civilisation*. London, Harrap, 1926.
Blinzler, J., *The Trial of Jesus*. Cork, Mercier; Westminster, Md., Newman, 1959.
Bonhoeffer, D., 'Die Kirche vor der Judenfrage' ('The Church in Face of the Jewish Question'), in *Gesammelte Schriften* ('Collected Works'), 4 vols, vol. 2. Munich 1958–61.
Bonsirven, J., *Palestinian Judaism at the Time of Jesus Christ*. New York, Holt, Rinehart, and Winston, 1963.
— *On the Ruins of the Temple*. London, Burns & Oates, 1931.
Bornkamm, G., *Jesus of Nazareth*. London, Hodder & Stoughton; New York, Harper, 1960.
Bousset, W. and Gressmann, H., *Die Religion des Judentums im späthellenistischen Zeitalter* ('The Religion of Judaism in the late Hellenistic Period'). Tübingen 1926.
Braun, H., *Jesus. Der Mann aus Nazareth und seine Zeit* ('Jesus. The Man from Nazareth and His Time'). Stuttgart 1969.

Brown, R. E., Fitzmyer, J. A., and Murphy, R. E., eds, *The Jerome Biblical Commentary*. 2 vols. Englewood Cliffs, Prentice Hall, 1968; London, Geoffrey Chapman, 1969.

Bultmann, R., *Theology of the New Testament*. 2 vols. London, SCM; New York, Scribner's, 1952.

— *Glauben und Vertstehen* ('Faith and Understanding'). 4 vols. Tübingen 1933–65.

— 'Prophecy and Fulfilment', in *Essays on Old Testament Interpretation*, ed. C. Westermann. London, SCM; Richmond, Va., John Knox, 1963.

— *Jesus and the Word*. London and New York, Scribner's, 1934.

Caird, G. B., *The Gospel of St. Luke*. Pelican Gospel Commentaries. Baltimore, Penguin, 1963; Harmondsworth, Penguin, 1971.

Dalman, G., *Christentum und Judentum* ('Christianity and Judaism'). Berlin 1898.

Davies, W. D., *Invitation to the New Testament*. New York, Doubleday, 1966; London, Darton, Longman & Todd, 1967.

Dibelius, M., *Botschaft und Geschichte* ('Message and History'). 2 vols. Tübingen 1956.

— *Jesus*. Philadelphia, Westminster, 1949; London, SCM, 1963.

Fenton, J. C., *The Gospel of St. Matthew*. Pelican Gospel Commentaries. Baltimore, Penguin, 1963; Harmondsworth, Penguin, 1968.

Fohrer, G., *Studien zur alttestamentlichen Theologie und Geschichte 1949–1966* ('Studies in Old Testament Theology and History 1949–1966'). Berlin, 1969.

— *History of Israelite Religion*. Nashville, Abingdon, 1972; London, SPCK, 1973.

Förster, W., *Palestinian Judaism in New Testament Times* (U.S. title *From the Exile to Christ: Historical Introduction to Palestinian Judaism*). Edinburgh, Oliver & Boyd; Philadelphia, Fortress, 1964.

Goguel, M., *Jesus and the Origins of Christianity*. 2 vols. New York, Harper Torchbooks, 1960. (ET of *Jésus*. Paris 1950.)

Goppelt, L., *Christentum und Judentum im ersten und zweiten*

Jahrhundert ('Christianity and Judaism in the First and Second Centuries'). Gütersloh 1954. A revised ET of the first half has appeared: *Jesus, Paul and Judaism*. New York, Thomas Nelson, 1964.

— *Christologie und Ethik* ('Christology and Ethics'). Göttingen, 1968.

Grundmann, W., *Die Geschichte Jesu Christi* ('The History of Jesus Christ'). Berlin, 1963.

Guardini, R., *The Lord*. Chicago, Regnery, 1954; London, Longmans Green, 1956.

Harnack, A. von, *Marcion*. Leipzig, 1921.

Hunter, A. M., *The Works and Words of Jesus*. London, SCM, 1973.

Jeremias, J., *The Parables of Jesus*. London, SCM, 1963; New York, Scribner's, 1972 (2nd rev. edn).

— *Jerusalem in the Time of Jesus*. Philadelphia, Fortress, 1967; London, SCM, 1969.

— *New Testament Theology: The Proclamation of Jesus*. London, SCM; New York, Scribner's, 1971.

Jones, A., *The Gospel According to St. Matthew*. London, Geoffrey Chapman; New York, Sheed & Ward, 1965.

Käsemann, E., *Exegetische Versuche und Besinnungen*. 2 vols. Göttingen, 1964. (ET: Vol. 1, *Essays on New Testament Themes*. London, SCM, 1964; Vol. 2, *New Testament Questions for Today*. Philadelphia, Fortress; London, SCM, 1969.)

Kee, H. C. and Young, F. W., *The Living World of the New Testament* (U.S. title *Understanding the New Testament*). London, Darton, Longman & Todd, 1960; Englewood Cliffs, Prentice-Hall, 1965 (2nd rev. edn).

Kittel, G., *Die Probleme des palästinensischen Spätjudentums und des Urchristentums* ('The Problems of Palestinian Late Judaism and of Primitive Christianity'). Stuttgart, 1926, 1948.

Kittel, R., *Die Religion des Volkes Israel* ('The Religion of the People of Israel'). 3 vols. Leipzig, 1921.

Kümmel, W. G., 'Die Gottesverkündigung Jesu und der Gottesgedanke des Spätjudentums' ('Jesus' Proclamation of

God and the Idea of God in Late Judaism'). *Judaica*, March 1945.

Kuss, O., *Auslegung und Verkündigung* ('Interpretation and Proclamation'). 2 vols. Regensburg, 1967.

Ladd, G. E., *Jesus and the Kingdom*. New York, Harper, 1964; London, SPCK, 1966.

Lagrange, M.-J., *Le Messianisme chez les Juifs*. Paris, 1909.

— *Le Judaïsme avant Jésus-Christ*. Paris, 1931.

Leipoldt, J. and Grundmann, W., eds., *Umwelt des Urchristentums* ('The Environment of Early Christianity'). 3 vols. Berlin, 1965.

Léon-Dufour, X., *Dictionary of Biblical Theology*. London, Geoffrey Chapman; New York, Desclee, 1967.

Lohfink, N., *The Christian Meaning of the Old Testament*. London, Burns & Oates; Milwaukee, Bruce, 1969.

Lohse, E., *Israel und die Christenheit* ('Israel and Christendom'). Göttingen, 1960.

— *History of the Suffering and Death of Jesus Christ*. Philadelphia, Fortress, 1967.

McKenzie, J. L., *Dictionary of the Bible*. New York, Macmillan, 1965; London, Geoffrey Chapman, 1966.

Manson, T. W., *The Teaching of Jesus*. Cambridge, Cambridge University Press, 1955.

Manson, W., *Jesus the Messiah*. London, Hodder & Stoughton, 1943; Philadelphia, Westminster, 1946.

Marquardt, F.-W., *Die Entdeckung des Judentums für die christliche Theologie* ('The Discovery of Judaism for Christian Theology'). Munich, 1967.

Marsh, J., *The Gospel of St. John*. Pelican New Testament Commentaries. Harmondsworth, Penguin; Baltimore, Penguin, 1968.

Meyer, E., *Ursprung und Anfänge des Christentums* ('The Origins and Beginnings of Christianity'). 3 vols. Berlin, 1921.

Montefiore, C. G., *The Synoptic Gospels*. 2 vols. 2nd rev. edn. London, Macmillan, 1927.

Montefiore, C. G. and Loewe, H., *A Rabbinic Anthology*. London, Macmillan, 1938; Cleveland and New York, World and Meridian Books, 1963.

Moore, G. F., 'Christian Writers on Judaism', *Harvard Theological Review*, July 1921.

— *Judaism in the First Centuries of the Christian Era, the Age of the Tannaim.* 3 vols. Cambridge, Mass., Harvard University Press, 1954.

Nineham, D. E., *The Gospel of St. Mark.* Pelican New Testament Commentaries. Baltimore, Penguin, 1964; Harmondsworth, Penguin, 1971.

Noth, M. *The History of Israel.* 2nd edn. London, A. & C. Black; New York, Harper, 1960.

— *The Laws in the Pentateuch and Other Studies.* Edinburgh, Oliver & Boyd, 1966; Philadelphia, Fortress, 1967.

Perrin, N., *The Kingdom of God in the Teaching of Jesus.* London, SCM; Philadelphia, Westminster, 1963.

— *Rediscovering the Teaching of Jesus.* London, SCM; New York, Harper, 1967.

Rahner, K., *Spiritual Exercises.* London and New York, Sheed & Ward, 1967.

Reumann, J. H. P., *Jesus in the Church's Gospels.* Philadelphia, Fortress, 1968; London, SPCK, 1970.

Robert, A. and Feuillet, A., eds., *Introduction to the New Testament.* New York, Seabury, 1968.

Schelkle, K. H., *Theologie des Neuen Testaments* ('Theology of the New Testament'). 3 vols. Düsseldorf, 1970.

Schiwy, G., *Der Weg ins Neue Testament* ('The Way into the New Testament'). 4 vols. Würzburg, 1965–70.

Schlier, H., *Die Zeit der Kirche* ('The Time of the Church'). Freiburg, 1962.

— *The Relevance of the New Testament.* London, Burns & Oates; New York, Herder & Herder, 1968.

Schmaus, M., *Katholische Dogmatik.* 8 vols. Munich 1958–63. An English translation is now appearing: *Dogma*, ed. T. Patrick Burke, London, Sheed & Ward; Mission, Kan., Sheed Andrews & McMeel, 1968.

— *Der Glaube der Kirche* ('The Faith of the Church'). 2 vols. Munich, 1969–70.

Schubert, K., ed., *Vom Messias zum Christus* ('From the Messiah to Christ'). Freiburg, 1964.

Schürer, E., *The History of the Jewish People in the Age of Jesus Christ*. Rev. edn, vol. i, ed. G. Vermes and F. Millar. Edinburgh, T. & T. Clark, 1973. (Complete edn, 3 vols, Edinburgh, T. & T. Clark, 1901–11.)

Stauffer, E., *New Testament Theology*. London, SCM; New York, Macmillan, 1955.

— *Jesus: Gestalt und Geschichte* ('Jesus: Form and History'). Bern, 1957.

Strack, H. L. and Billerbeck, P., *Kommentar zum Neuen Testament aus Talmud und Midrasch* ('Commentary on the New Testament from Talmud and Midrash'). 6 vols. Munich, 1922–61.

Tillich, P., *Systematic Theology*, vol. ii. London, Nisbet; Chicago, University of Chicago Press, 1957.

Wellhausen, J., *Israelitische und jüdische Geschichte* ('Israelite and Jewish History'). Berlin, 1914.

Westermann, C., *The Old Testament and Jesus Christ*. Minneapolis, Augsburg, 1970.

Zimmerli, W., 'Promise and Fulfilment', in *Essays on Old Testament Interpretation*, ed. C. Westermann. London, SCM; Richmond, Va., John Knox, 1963.